THE RIVALS

Crofts Classics

GENERAL EDITORS

Samuel H. Beer, *Harvard University*

O. B. Hardison, Jr., *The Folger Shakespeare Library*

RICHARD BRINSLEY SHERIDAN

The
Rivals

EDITED BY

Alan S. Downer

Harlan Davidson, Inc.
Arlington Heights, Illinois 60004

ISBN: 0-88295-091-6
(Formerly 0-390-23944-5)

Library of Congress Card Number: 52-13686

82   83   84   85CB18   17   16   15

INTRODUCTION

VERY FEW of the plays written and produced in the busy theaters of eighteenth-century England have any more than antiquarian interest today. It is therefore somewhat surprising to find that three of the classics of English comedy (classics in the sense that they have been read with delight and revived with success for nearly two centuries) were written by two men between 1773 and 1777. Oliver Goldsmith, author of *She Stoops to Conquer,* and Richard Brinsley Sheridan, author of *The Rivals* and *The School for Scandal,* had several things in common. They were not playwrights by profession: Goldsmith was a doctor, Sheridan a politician and theater-manager. And they shared what was for their time a radical attitude about the nature of stage comedy.

In the early years of the century, under the leadership of men like Sir Richard Steele (co-editor of the *Tatler* and *Spectator* papers) comic writers had been turned in the direction of sentimentality, humanitarianism, and moralizing. Comedy is, of course, fundamentally as didactic as tragedy, but in other eras it had done its teaching with gaiety and good humor, and with boisterous or subtle satire. Steele's comedies, for all their solemn moralizing, manage to retain some of the spirit of laughter, but his followers succumbed completely to the middle-class demand that the theater be a source of improvement, substituting moral saws for epigrams and pathos for ridicule. In Sheridan's burlesque play, *The Critic,* a manuscript is identified as being a comedy when a reader discovers the stage direction, *"Bursts into tears, and exit."*

Goldsmith and Sheridan were almost alone in their desire to return comedy to its old purpose of teaching by laughter. Goldsmith had a rousing success with *She Stoops to Conquer;* Sheridan's first contribution to the cause, *The Rivals,* was, at its initial performance, less successful. (See page xi below, under the year 1775.) In his Preface, Sheridan attributes his failure to the fact that he was "not conversant with plays in general." He had not had enough experience in the theater, he claims, and did not know enough plays, to recognize what would and would not go down with an audience.

At best, this is a half-truth. *The Rivals* is in large part made up of standard comic elements, and it even contains direct references to particular well-known plays. The standard elements will be considered later, but it may be pointed out at once that the challenge scene and duel echo similar incidents in Shakespeare's *Twelfth Night,* while servant David speaking of honor is reminiscent of Falstaff. Sheridan was acquainted with Restoration Comedy, since he adapted the works of Congreve and Vanbrugh to the primmer tastes of the eighteenth-century audience; he knew the sentimental comedy of his own time, because he burlesqued it; he was well read in Shakespeare since he quotes and borrows incidents from him. But that Sheridan uses the traditional materials of comedy does not diminish the stature of his own achievement. "True wit," as Alexander Pope declared with finality, is based on that which "oft was thought, but ne'er so well expressed."

In understanding and assessing a work written according to Pope's critical theory, the first step is to discover the standard comic materials employed by the author. The second, and more important, is to examine the use he makes of such materials. An analysis of the structure, the characterization, the dialogue of *The Rivals* will reveal its purpose, and perhaps the reasons for its continuing success.

Sheridan returns to the traditions of Restoration Comedy for his structure, the pattern of his action. The plot is extremely complex, with disguises piled on disguises, the machinations of several clever servants, and the intricate exposure of several aspects of human folly at once. This complexity is apt to confuse *readers* in a way that Sheridan never intended, for the effect of the play in the theater is of a series of brilliantly comic scenes to be enjoyed in and of themselves, without too much concern for the relationship between the parts of the whole. It is sufficient for the *spectator* that the tendency of all the scenes is the same, to expose the follies of mankind, without worrying about a dominant pattern of action. The pattern is there, of course, but the wise reader will not allow himself to be troubled by the labyrinthine mechanics of the plot. The important thing is the comic aspect of the moment— the whole will take care of itself.

The Rivals adopts the oldest tradition of comedy; instead of moralizing on human behavior, it satirizes manners. The scene, the city of Bath and its environs, was as well known to the London audience as that of a nearby summer resort might be to a modern metropolitan audience. Sheridan makes dramatic capital of the facts of life in Bath, that duelling was forbidden within the city, for instance, and that there were convenient spots outside the city where duels might take place. He refers to familiar places, like the North Promenade and the New Rooms, to create the effect of actuality. Then, having established the "normalcy" of the world of his play, he proceeds to satirize the preoccupations of that world. He pokes fun at current best-sellers; he ridicules social pretension in the behavior of the servants. The whole characterization of Lydia Languish is a frontal attack on the false values of sentimental romanticism.

Sheridan's men and women are mostly "humour" characters. That is, they belong to those comic types who are governed by a single passion or attitude or quirk, usually indicated by their names. Acres is a countryman, Mrs. Malaprop misuses the language, Sir Anthony is "absolute in everything." Other characters are drawn from the stock types of comedy: Sir Lucius is the stage Irishman, loquacious and belligerent; Fag and David are "clever servants." On the other hand, Sheridan pokes fun at the humour of the heroine of sentimental comedy, and rejects the hero almost completely. Lydia Languish *would like* to be like her name, but she is not; and the hero only appears to be a rake. He is actually in control of the situation throughout, and not so much witty as wise.

The play, to be sure, has its faults. The exposition is huddled and careless. The servants in the opening scene set forth the situation in a brazen manner that no modern audience would tolerate. Much of the action is motivated by eavesdropping, and the division into acts is not based on climaxes in the plot, but the necessities of the theater. And however much Sheridan may pretend that his comedy does not moralize, the scenes between Julia and Faulkland argue against him. But in production the virtues far outweigh the faults. The conventional motivations lead to situations of great comic delight, and the care with which even the most minor figure has been drawn has made this the most popular of plays for "all star" revivals.

However dated the manners and morals, however stereotyped the characters, *The Rivals* is full of the gusto of a young playwright who enjoyed life and found humanity funny and exhilarating. Mrs. Malaprop's small pride in her parts of speech ridicules the semiliteracy which, our recent semanticists have solemnly discovered, creates the basic misunderstandings by which we live. Lydia's wish to be swept away by a grand passion is a comic echo of the dreams of half of mankind. Even Faulkland's posturing, his effort to find emotional satisfaction in melodramatizing every situation in which he finds himself, can be related to universal motives revealed in the case histories collated by serious students of psychology. But Sheridan would doubtless reject both psychoanalysis and semantics as unnecessarily complicated methods of teaching and reform.

Sheridan chooses the older method of *castigans ridendo,* of pedagogy by laughter and ridicule. This is a method not wholly in favor today, since we have come to believe that ridicule is somehow inhumane, and to employ it may invite the risk of more serious consequences. Sheridan's ridicule, of course, hurts no one and never has. It is not that Lucy and Mrs. Malaprop and Acres are so remote from life that they may be observed distantly like the caricatures of farce. They represent facets of humanity in general and the laughter they arouse is affectionate, for Sheridan is making us laugh at our own dreams, our own small follies. If we can laugh at our dreams, we may be less disappointed when they fail to materialize; if we laugh at our own follies we may develop a greater tolerance for the follies of others. And that is, perhaps, the secret of the long life of *The Rivals.*

The text of this edition has been collated with the third edition (London, 1776), the last revised by Sheridan. The original version of the stage direction at Faulkland's entrance in Act V, which appears in the manuscript and the early editions but is dropped in the third, has, however, been retained, since it clarifies the somewhat mysterious behavior of the young man during the rest of the scene. The punctuation of the original text has been modified for the assistance of the modern reader to eliminate ambiguities. Wherever possible, however, the eighteenth-century dramatic convention of a liberal use of the dash has been retained: it preserves some of the flavor of the original performance, suggesting the style of comic delivery then popular—breaking speeches and changing tone and tempo to underline the wit—and, where wit was lacking, to provide a reasonable facsimile through the actor's vocalism. For the most part, the language of the play is sufficiently modern to require few glosses, and the reader is surely entitled to the pleasure of exposing, from his own superior knowledge of the English language, the blunders of Mrs. Malaprop.

PRINCIPAL DATES IN SHERIDAN'S LIFE

1751. Richard Brinsley Sheridan born in Dublin, October 30. His father, Thomas, was an actor-manager and teacher of elocution; his mother, Frances, was a minor novelist and playwright.

1770. Family settled in Bath, England, and became acquainted with Linley, a musician, and his family.

1771-1773. Sheridan published occasional verses and collaborated on an unproduced farce, *Jupiter*.

1772. Eloped with Miss Linley, to protect her from the unwelcome advances of Major Matthews. Leaving her in France, Sheridan returned to Bath and fought two duels with the aggrieved major.

1773. Married Miss Linley.

1775. *The Rivals*, first produced at Covent Garden Theater on January 17 with no success, was revised and presented at the same theater on January 28 to great acclaim. This was followed on May 2nd by a short farce, *St. Patrick's Day, or The Scheming Lieutenant*, written by Sheridan for the benefit of Clinch, the original actor of Sir Lucius O'Trigger. On November 21, Sheridan's comic opera, *The Duenna*, began an unprecedented run of 75 nights.

1776. In partnership with Linley and Ford succeeded David Garrick as manager of Drury Lane Theater.

1777. Presented *A Trip to Scarborough*, his own adaptation of Vanbrugh's comedy, *The Relapse*, on February 24. In March, on the motion of Dr. Johnson, he was elected a member of the famous Literary Club. *The School for Scandal*, Sheridan's most successful play, was first presented on May 8.

1779. *The Critic*, a burlesque of theatrical fads and conventions, was produced on October 29.

1780. Became Member of Parliament for Stafford.

1787. Delivered, on February 7, his first speech against Warren Hastings, a landmark in parliamentary oratory.

1799. Presented his last play, *Pizarro*, a melodrama adapted from the German, on May 24.

1809. Burning of Drury Lane Theater led to financial difficulties.

1813. Arrested for debt as a consequence of his losses in the theater fire.

1816. Died in London, July 7. Accorded a great public funeral, and buried in Westminster Abbey.

THE RIVALS

PREFACE

A PREFACE to a play seems generally to be considered as a kind of closet-prologue,[1] in which—if his piece has been successful—the author solicits that indulgence from the reader which he had before experienced from the audience: but as the scope and immediate object of a play is to please a mixed assembly in *representation* (whose judgment in the theatre at least is decisive), its degree of reputation is usually as determined by the public, before it can be prepared for the cooler tribunal of the study. Thus any further solicitude on the part of the writer becomes unnecessary at least, if not an intrusion: and if the piece has been condemned in the performance, I fear an address to the closet, like an appeal to posterity, is constantly regarded as the procrastination of a suit, from a consciousness of the weakness of the cause. From these considerations, the following comedy would certainly have been submitted to the reader, without any further introduction than what it had in the representation, but that its success has probably been founded on a circumstance which the author is informed has not before attended a theatrical trial, and which consequently ought not to pass unnoticed.

I need scarcely add, that the circumstance alluded to was the withdrawing of the piece, to remove those imperfections in the first representation which were too obvious to escape reprehension, and too numerous

[1] closet-prologue introduction for the reading public

to admit of a hasty correction. There are few writers, I believe, who, even in the fullest consciousness of error, do not wish to palliate the faults which they acknowledge; and, however trifling the performance, to second their confession of its deficiencies, by whatever plea seems least disgraceful to their ability. In the present instance, it cannot be said to amount either to candour or modesty in me, to acknowledge an extreme inexperience and want of judgment on matters, in which, without guidance from practice, or spur from success, a young man should scarcely boast of being an adept. If it be said that under such disadvantages no one should attempt to write a play, I must beg leave to dissent from the position, while the first point of experience that I have gained on the subject is a knowledge of the candour and judgment with which an impartial public distinguishes between the errors of inexperience and incapacity, and the indulgence which it shows even to a disposition to remedy the defects of either.

It were unnecessary to enter into any further extenuation of what was thought exceptionable in this play, but that it has been said, that the managers should have prevented some of the defects before its appearance to the public—and in particular the uncommon length of the piece as represented the first night. It were an ill return for the most liberal and gentlemanly conduct on their side, to suffer any censure to rest where none was deserved. Hurry in writing has long been exploded as an excuse for an author;—however, in the dramatic line, it may happen, that both an author and a manager may wish to fill a chasm in the entertainment of the public with a hastiness not altogether culpable. The season was advanced when I first put the play into Mr. Harris's[2] hands: it was at that time at least double the length of any acting

[2] Mr. Harris Thomas Harris, manager of Covent Garden Theatre

comedy. I profited by his judgment and experience in the curtailing of it—till, I believe, his feeling for the vanity of a young author got the better of his desire for correctness, and he left many excrescences remaining, because he had assisted in pruning so many more. Hence, though I was not uninformed that the acts were still too long, I flattered myself that, after the first trial, I might with safer judgment proceed to remove what should appear to have been most dissatisfactory. Many other errors there were, which might in part have arisen from my being by no means conversant with plays in general, either in reading or at the theatre. Yet I own that, in one respect, I did not regret my ignorance: for as my first wish in attempting a play was to avoid every appearance of plagiary, I thought I should stand a better chance of effecting this from being in a walk which I had not frequented, and where, consequently, the progress of invention was less likely to be interrupted by starts of recollection: for on subjects on which the mind has been much informed, invention is slow of exerting itself. Faded ideas float in the fancy like half-forgotten dreams; and the imagination in its fullest enjoyments becomes suspicious of its offspring, and doubts whether it has created or adopted.

With regard to some particular passages which on the first night's representation seemed generally disliked, I confess that if I felt any emotion of surprise at the disapprobation, it was not that they were disapproved of, but that I had not before perceived that they deserved it. As some part of the attack on the piece was begun too early to pass for the sentence of *judgment*, which is ever tardy in condemning, it has been suggested to me that much of the disapprobation must have arisen from virulence of malice, rather than severity of criticism: but as I was more apprehensive of there being just grounds to excite the latter than

conscious of having deserved the former, I continue
not to believe that probable which I am sure must
have been unprovoked. However, if it was so, and I
could even mark the quarter from whence it came, it
would be ungenerous to retort; for no passion suffers
more than malice from disappointment. For my own
part, I see no reason why the author of a play should
not regard a first night's audience as a candid and judicious friend attending, in behalf of the public, at his
last rehearsal. If he can dispense with flattery, he is
sure at least of sincerity, and even though the annota-
tion be rude, he may rely upon the justness of the
comment. Considered in this light, that audience,
whose *fiat* is essential to the poet's claim, whether his
object be fame or profit, has surely a right to expect
some deference to its opinion, from principles of politeness at least, if not from gratitude.

As for the little puny critics, who scatter their pee-
vish strictures in private circles, and scribble at every
author who has the eminence of being unconnected
with them, as they are usually spleen-swoln from a vain
idea of increasing their consequence, there will always
be found a petulance and illiberality in their remarks,
which should place them as far beneath the notice of
a gentleman as their original dulness had sunk them
from the level of the most unsuccessful author.

It is not without pleasure that I catch at an opportunity of justifying myself from the charge of intending
any national reflection in the character of Sir Lucius
O'Trigger. If any gentlemen opposed the piece from
that idea, I thank them sincerely for their opposition;
and if the condemnation of this comedy (however
misconceived the provocation) could have added one
spark to the decaying flame of national attachment to
the country supposed to be reflected on, I should have
been happy in its fate, and might with truth have
boasted that it had done more real service in its failure

than the successful morality of a thousand stage-novels will ever effect.

It is usual, I believe, to thank the performers in a new play for the exertion of their several abilities. But where (as in this instance) their merit has been so striking and uncontroverted as to call for the warmest and truest applause from a number of judicious audiences, the poet's after-praise comes like the feeble acclamation of a child to close the shouts of a multitude. The conduct however, of the principals in a theatre cannot be so apparent to the public. I think it therefore but justice to declare, that from this theatre (the only one I can speak of from experience) those writers who wish to try the dramatic line will meet with that candour and liberal attention which are generally allowed to be better calculated to lead genius into excellence than either the precepts of judgment or the guidance of experience.

THE AUTHOR.

PROLOGUE

(*Enter* SERGEANT-AT-LAW,[1] *and* ATTORNEY *following,
and giving a paper*)

SERJEANT.   What's here!—a vile cramp hand![2] I
cannot see
Without my spectacles.
    ATTORNEY.   He means his fee.
Nay, Mr. Serjeant, good sir, try again.
                    (*Gives* [*him*] *money*)
    SERJEANT.   The scrawl improves! (*more*) O come,
'tis pretty plain.
Hey! how's this? Dibble!—sure it cannot be!
A poet's brief! a poet and a fee!
    ATTORNEY.   Yea, sir! though you without reward, I
know,
Would gladly plead the Muse's cause.
    SERJEANT.   So!—So!
    ATTORNEY.   And if the fee offends, your wrath
should fall
On me.
    SERJEANT.   Dear Dibble, no offence at all.
    ATTORNEY.   Some sons of Phœbus in the courts we
meet,
    SERJEANT.   And fifty sons of Phœbus in the Fleet![3]
    ATTORNEY.   Nor pleads he worse, who with a de-
cent sprig
Of bays[4] adorns his legal waste of wig.
    SERJEANT.   Full-bottomed heroes[5] thus, on signs,
unfurl

[1] Serjeant-at-law senior member of the bar   [2] hand handwriting
[3] Fleet debtor's prison   [4] bays laurel wreath, the badge of a
poet   [5] Full-bottomed heroes lawyers wearing oversized wigs

A leaf of laurel in a grove of curl!
Yet tell your client, that, in adverse days,
This wig is warmer than a bush of bays.

   ATTORNEY. Do you, then, sir, my client's place
     supply,
Profuse of robe, and prodigal of tie——
Do you, with all those blushing powers of face,⎤
And wonted bashful hesitating grace,   ⎬
Rise in the court and flourish on the case. ⎦

                              (*Exit*)

   SERJEANT. For practice then suppose—this brief
     will show it,—
Me, Serjeant Woodward,—counsel for the poet.
Used to the ground, I know 'tis hard to deal
With this dread court,[6] from whence there's no ap-
     peal;
No tricking here, to blunt the edge of law,
Or, damn'd in equity, escape by flaw:
But judgment given, your sentence must remain;
No writ of error[7] lies—to Drury-lane! [8]
   Yet when so kind you seem, 'tis past dispute
We gain some favour, if not costs of suit.
No spleen is here! I see no hoarded fury;—
I think I never faced a milder jury!
Sad else our plight! where frowns are transportation,[9]
A hiss the gallows, and a groan damnation!
But such the public candour, without fear
My client waives all right of challenge here.
No newsman from our session is dismiss'd,
Nor wit nor critic we scratch off the list;
His faults can never hurt another's ease,
His crime, at worst, a bad attempt to please:
Thus, all respecting, he appeals to all,
And by the general voice will stand or fall.

[6] this dread court the audience   [7] writ of error appeal   [8] Drury-lane the competing theater [9] transportation i.e. to the penal settlements in the colonies, hence a sentence of exile

PROLOGUE

SPOKEN [ON THE TENTH NIGHT] BY MRS. BULKLEY

GRANTED our cause, our suit and trial o'er,
The worthy serjeant need appear no more:
In pleasing I a different client choose,
He served the Poet—I would serve the Muse.
Like him, I'll try to merit your applause,
A female counsel in a female's cause.
   Look on this form,[10]—where humour, quaint and
     sly,
Dimples the cheek, and points the beaming eye:
Where gay invention seems to boast its wiles
In amorous hint, and half-triumphant smiles;
While her light mask or covers satire's strokes,
Or[11] hides the conscious blush her wit provokes.
Look on her well—does she seem form'd to teach?
Should you expect to hear this lady preach?
Is grey experience suited to her youth?
Do solemn sentiments become that mouth?
Bid her be grave, those lips should rebel prove
To every theme that slanders mirth or love.
   Yet, thus adorn'd with every graceful art
To charm the fancy and yet reach the heart——
Must we displace her, and instead advance
The goddess of the woful countenance—
The sentimental Muse?—Her emblems view,
The Pilgrim's Progress, and a sprig of rue!
View her—too chaste to look like flesh and blood—
Primly portray'd on emblematic wood!
There, fix'd in usurpation, should she stand,
She'll snatch the dagger from her sister's[12] hand:

[10] this form "Pointing to the figure of Comedy" at one side of the proscenium arch   [11] or . . . or either . . . or   [12] sister's the Muse of Tragedy

And having made her votaries weep a flood,
Good heaven! she'll end her comedies in blood—
Bid Harry Woodward break poor Dunstal's[13] crown,
Imprison Quick, and knock Ned Shuter down;
While sad Barsanti, weeping o'er the scene,
Shall stab herself—or poison Mrs. Green.
 Such dire encroachments to prevent in time,
Demands the critic's voice—the poet's rhyme.
Can our light scenes add strength to holy laws!
Such puny patronage but hurts the cause:
Fair virtue scorns our feeble aid to ask;
And moral truth disdains the trickster's mask.
For here their favourite stands,[14] whose brow, severe
And sad, claims youth's respect, and pity's tear;
Who, when oppress'd by foes her worth creates,
Can point a poniard at the guilt she hates.

[13] Dunstal . . . Quick . . . Shuter . . . Barsanti . . . Mrs. Green actors of comedy
[14] For here . . . stands "Pointing to [the figure of] Tragedy" at the other side of the proscenium

DRAMATIS PERSONAE

As Originally Acted at Covent-Garden Theatre in 1775

SIR ANTHONY ABSOLUTE	*Mr. Shuter.*
CAPTAIN ABSOLUTE	*Mr. Woodward.*
FAULKLAND	*Mr. Lewis.*
ACRES	*Mr. Quick.*
SIR LUCIUS O'TRIGGER	*Mr. Lee.*
FAG	*Mr. Lee Lewes.*
DAVID	*Mr. Dunstal*
THOMAS	*Mr. Fearon.*
MRS. MALAPROP	*Mrs. Green.*
LYDIA LANGUISH	*Miss Barsanti.*
JULIA	*Mrs. Bulkley.*
LUCY	*Mrs. Lessingham.*

Maid, Boy, Servants, &c.

SCENE: *Bath.*
Time of Action—Five Hours.

THE RIVALS

❀

Act I

SCENE I: *A Street* [*in Bath*]

(*Enter* THOMAS; *he crosses the Stage;* FAG *follows, looking after him*)

FAG. What! Thomas! Sure 'tis he?—What! Thomas! Thomas!

THOMAS. Hey!—Odd's[1] life! Mr. Fag!—give us your hand, my old fellow-servant.

FAG. Excuse my glove, Thomas:—I'm devilish glad to see you, my lad. Why, my prince of charioteers, you look as hearty!—but who the deuce thought of seeing you in Bath?

THOMAS. Sure, Master, Madam Julia, Harry, Mrs. Kate, and the postilion, be all come.

FAG. Indeed!

THOMAS. Ay, Master thought another fit of the gout was coming to make him a visit; so he'd a mind to gi't the slip, and whip! we were all off at an hour's warning.

FAG. Ay, ay, hasty in everything, or it would not be Sir Anthony Absolute!

THOMAS. But tell us, Mr. Fag, how does young Master? Odd! Sir Anthony will stare to see the captain here!

FAG. I do not serve Captain Absolute now.

THOMAS. Why sure!

[1] Odd's God's

1

FAG. At present I am employed by Ensign Beverley.

THOMAS. I doubt,[2] Mr. Fag, you ha'n't changed for the better.

FAG. I have not changed, Thomas.

THOMAS. No! Why, didn't you say you had left young Master?

FAG. No.—Well, honest Thomas, I must puzzle you no farther:—briefly then—Captain Absolute and Ensign Beverley are one and the same person.

THOMAS. The devil they are!

FAG. So it is indeed, Thomas; and the *ensign* half of my master being on guard at present—the *captain* has nothing to do with me.

THOMAS. So, so!—What, this is some freak, I warrant!—Do tell us, Mr. Fag, the meaning o't—you know I ha' trusted you.

FAG. You'll be secret, Thomas?

THOMAS. As a coach-horse.

FAG. Why then the cause of all this is—LOVE,—Love, Thomas, who (as you may get read to you) has been a masquerader ever since the days of Jupiter.

THOMAS. Ay, ay;—I guessed there was a lady in the case:—but pray, why does your master pass only for an *ensign*?—Now if he had shammed *general* indeed——

FAG. Ah! Thomas, there lies the mystery o' the matter—Hark'ee, Thomas, my master is in love with a lady of a very singular taste: a lady who likes him better as a half-pay ensign than if she knew he was son and heir to Sir Anthony Absolute, a baronet with three thousand a-year!

THOMAS. That is an odd taste indeed!—But has she got the stuff, Mr. Fag? Is she rich, hey?

FAG. Rich!—Why, I believe she owns half the stocks! Zounds! Thomas, she could pay the national

[2] **doubt** fear

debt as easy as I could my washerwoman! She has a lap-dog that eats out of gold,—she feeds her parrot with small pearls,—and all her thread-papers are made of bank-notes!

THOMAS. Bravo, faith!—Odd! I warrant she has a set of thousands at least:—but does she draw kindly with the captain?

FAG. As fond as pigeons.

THOMAS. May one hear her name?

FAG. Miss Lydia Languish.—But there is an old tough aunt in the way; though, by-the-by, she has never seen my master—for we got acquainted with Miss while on a visit in Gloucestershire.

THOMAS. Well—I wish they were once harnessed together in matrimony.—But pray, Mr. Fag, what kind of a place is this Bath?—I ha' heard a deal of it—here's a mort[3] o' merry-making, hey?

FAG. Pretty well, Thomas, pretty well—'tis a good lounge;[4] in the morning we go to the pump-room (though neither my master nor I drink the waters); after breakfast we saunter on the parades or play a game at billiards; at night we dance; but damn the place, I'm tired of it: their regular hours stupefy me— not a fiddle nor a card after eleven!—However Mr. Faulkland's gentleman and I keep it up a little in private parties;—I'll introduce you there, Thomas—you'll like him much.

THOMAS. Sure I know Mr. Du-Peigne—you know his master is to marry Madam Julia.

FAG. I had forgot.—But, Thomas, you must polish a little—indeed you must.—Here now—this wig! What the devil do you do with a wig, Thomas?— None of the London whips[5] of any degree of *ton*[6] wear wigs now.

THOMAS. More's the pity! more's the pity! I say.—

[3] **mort** great quantity [4] **lounge** vacation spot [5] **whips** coachmen [6] **ton** stylishness

Odd's life! when I heard how the lawyers and doctors had took to their own hair, I thought how 'twould go next:—odd rabbit it![7] when the fashion had got foot on the bar, I guessed 'twould mount to the box!—but 'tis all out of character, believe me, Mr. Fag: and look'ee, I'll never gi' up mine—the lawyers and doctors may do as they will.

FAG. Well, Thomas, we'll not quarrel about that.

THOMAS. Why, bless you, the gentlemen of the professions ben't all of a mind—for in our village now, tho'ff[8] Jack Gauge, the exciseman, has ta'en to his carrots, there's little Dick the farrier swears he'll never forsake his bob, though all the college should appear with their own heads!

FAG. Indeed! well said, Dick!—but hold—mark! mark! Thomas.

THOMAS. Zooks! 'tis the captain.—Is that the lady with him?

FAG. No no, that is Madam Lucy, my master's mistress's maid. They lodge at that house—but I must after him to tell him the news.

THOMAS. Odd! he's giving her money!—Well, Mr. Fag——

FAG. Good-bye, Thomas. I have an appointment in Gyde's Porch[9] this evening at eight; meet me there, and we'll make a little party.   (*Exeunt severally*)[10]

SCENE II: *A Dressing-room in* MRS. MALAPROP'S *Lodgings*

(LYDIA *sitting on a sofa, with a book in her hand.* LUCY, *as just returned from a message.*)[1]

LUCY. Indeed, ma'am, I traversed half the town in

[7] **odd rabbit it** doggone it (like most of the "oaths" in this play a meaningless exclamation)   [8] **tho'ff** though   [9] **Gyde's Porch** Assembly rooms   [10] **severally** in different directions   [1] **message** errand

search of it! I don't believe there's a circulating library in Bath I han't been at.

LYDIA. And could not you get *The Reward of Constancy?* [2]

LUCY. No, indeed, ma'am.

LYDIA. Nor *The Fatal Connection?* [3]

LUCY. No, indeed, ma'am.

LYDIA. Nor *The Mistakes of the Heart?* [4]

LUCY. Ma'am, as ill luck would have it, Mr. Bull said Miss Sukey Saunter had just fetched it away.

LYDIA. Heigh-ho! Did you inquire for *The Delicate Distress*—

LUCY. Or, *The Memoirs of Lady Woodford?* [5] Yes, indeed, ma'am. I asked everywhere for it; and I might have brought it from Mr. Frederick's, but Lady Slattern Lounger, who had just sent it home, had so soiled and dog's-eared [6] it, it wa'n't fit for a Christian to read.

LYDIA. Heigh-ho! Yes, I always know when Lady Slattern has been before me. She has a most observing thumb; and, I believe, cherishes her nails for the convenience of making marginal notes.—Well, child, what *have* you brought me?

LUCY. Oh! here, ma'am.—(*Taking books from under her cloak and from her pockets*) This is *The Gordian Knot*,[7]—and this *Peregrine Pickle*.[8] Here are *The Tears of Sensibility*,[9] and *Humphrey Clinker*.[10] This is *The Memoirs of a Lady of Quality, written by Her-*

[2] *The Reward of Constancy* an unidentified sentimental novel [3] *The Fatal Connection* a two-volume novel by Mrs. Fogarty, 1773 [4] *The Mistakes of the Heart* a romance of "high life" by Treyssac de Vergy, 1769 [5] *The Delicate Distress, or the Memoirs of Lady Woodford* by Elizabeth Griffin, 1769. Sheridan implies that the four books most desired by Lydia are sensational love stories of the sort found today in "true confession" magazines [6] *dog's-eared* marked the place by turning down the corners of pages [7] *The Gordian Knot* by Elizabeth Griffin, 1769 [8] *Peregrine Pickle* by Tobias Smollett, 1751 [9] *The Tears of Sensibility*, translated from the French of Baculard d'Arnaud, 1773 [10] *Humphrey Clinker*, by Smollett, 1771

self,[11] and here the second volume of *The Sentimental Journey.*[12]

LYDIA.   Heigh-ho!—What are those books by the glass?

LUCY.   The great one is only *The Whole Duty of Man*[13]—where I press a few blonds,[14] ma'am.

LYDIA.   Very well—give me the sal volatile.

LUCY.   Is it in a blue cover, ma'am?

LYDIA.   My smelling-bottle, you simpleton!

LUCY.   Oh, the drops—here, ma'am.

LYDIA.   Hold!—here's some one coming—quick! see who it is.—(*Exit* LUCY) Surely I heard my cousin Julia's voice.

(*Re-enter* LUCY)

LUCY.   Lud! ma'am, here is Miss Melville.
LYDIA.   Is it possible?—   (*Exit* LUCY)

(*Enter* JULIA)

LYDIA.   My dearest Julia, how delighted am I!— (*Embrace*) How unexpected was this happiness!

JULIA.   True, Lydia—and our pleasure is the greater.—But what has been the matter?—you were denied to me at first!

LYDIA.   Ah, Julia, I have a thousand things to tell you!—But first inform me what has conjured you to Bath?—Is Sir Anthony here?

JULIA.   He is—we are arrived within this hour— and I suppose he will be here to wait on Mrs. Malaprop as soon as he is dressed.

LYDIA.   Then before we are interrupted, let me im-

[11] *The Memoirs of a Lady of Quality,* by Lady Vane (incorporated into *Peregrine Pickle*), 1751   [12] *The Sentimental Journey,* by Laurence Sterne, 1768. Lucy has been able to get from Mr. Frederick (an actual bookseller of Bath) only a disappointing collection of old, or incomplete, or highly moral novels   [13] *The Whole Duty of Man* an extremely popular book of commonplace moralizing   [14] **blonds** bits of lace

part to you some of my distress!—I know your gentle nature will sympathize with me, though your prudence may condemn me! My letters have informed you of my whole connection with Beverley; but I have lost him, Julia! My aunt has discovered our intercourse by a note she intercepted, and has confined me ever since! Yet, would you believe it? she has absolutely fallen in love with a tall Irish baronet she met one night since she has been here, at Lady Macshuffle's rout.[15]

JULIA. You jest, Lydia!

LYDIA. No, upon my word.—She really carries on a kind of correspondence with him, under a feigned name though, till she chooses to be known to him: but it is a *Delia* or a *Celia*, I assure you.

JULIA. Then, surely, she is now more indulgent to her niece.

LYDIA. Quite the contrary. Since she has discovered her own frailty, she is become more suspicious of mine. Then I must inform you of another plague! That odious Acres is to be in Bath to-day: so that I protest I shall be teased out of all spirits!

JULIA. Come, come, Lydia, hope the best—Sir Anthony shall use his interest with Mrs. Malaprop.

LYDIA. But you have not heard the worst. Unfortunately I had quarrelled with my poor Beverley, just before my aunt made the discovery, and I have not seen him since to make it up.

JULIA. What was his offence?

LYDIA. Nothing at all! But, I don't know how it was, as often as we had been together, we had never had a quarrel, and, somehow, I was afraid he would never give me an opportunity. So, last Thursday, I wrote a letter to myself, to inform myself that Beverley was at that time paying his addresses to another woman. I signed it *your friend unknown*, showed it to Beverley, charged him with his falsehood, put myself

[15] **rout** large evening party, reception

in a violent passion, and vowed I'd never see him more.

JULIA.   And you let him depart so, and have not seen him since?

LYDIA.   'Twas the next day my aunt found the matter out. I intended only to have teased him three days and a half, and now I've lost him for ever.

JULIA.   If he is as deserving and sincere as you have represented him to me, he will never give you up so. Yet consider, Lydia, you tell me he is but an ensign, and you have thirty thousand pounds.

LYDIA.   But you know I lose most of my fortune if I marry without my aunt's consent, till of age; and that is what I have determined to do, ever since I knew the penalty. Nor could I love the man who would wish to wait a day for the alternative.

JULIA.   Nay, this is caprice!

LYDIA.   What, does Julia tax me with caprice? I thought her lover Faulkland had inured her to it.

JULIA.   I do not love even *his* faults.

LYDIA.   But *àpropos*[16]—you have sent to him, I suppose?

JULIA.   Not yet, upon my word—nor has he the least idea of my being in Bath. Sir Anthony's resolution was so sudden, I could not inform him of it.

LYDIA.   Well, Julia, you are your own mistress (though under the protection of Sir Anthony), yet have you, for this long year, been a slave to the caprice, the whim, the jealousy of this ungrateful Faulkland, who will ever delay assuming the right of a husband, while you suffer him to be equally imperious as a lover.

JULIA.   Nay, you are wrong entirely. We were contracted before my father's death. *That,* and some consequent embarrassments, have delayed what I know to be my Faulkland's most ardent wish. He is too generous to trifle on such a point.—And for his character,

[16] *àpropos* in that connection

you wrong him there, too. No, Lydia, he is too proud, too noble, to be jealous; if he is captious, 'tis without dissembling; if fretful, without rudeness. Unused to the fopperies of love, he is negligent of the little duties expected from a lover—but being unhackneyed in the passion, his affection is ardent and sincere; and as it engrosses his whole soul, he expects every thought and emotion of his mistress to move in unison with his. Yet, though his pride calls for this full return, his humility makes him undervalue those qualities in him which would entitle him to it; and not feeling why he should be loved to the degree he wishes, he still suspects that he is not loved enough. This temper, I must own, has cost me many unhappy hours; but I have learned to think myself his debtor for those imperfections which arise from the ardour of his attachment.

Lydia. Well, I cannot blame you for defending him. But tell me candidly, Julia, had he never saved your life, do you think you should have been attached to him as you are?—Believe me, the rude blast that overset your boat was a prosperous gale of love to him.

Julia. Gratitude may have strengthened my attachment to Mr. Faulkland, but I loved him before he had preserved me; yet surely that alone were an obligation sufficient.

Lydia. Obligation!—why a water spaniel would have done as much!—Well, I should never think of giving my heart to a man because he could swim!

Julia. Come, Lydia, you are too inconsiderate.

Lydia. Nay, I do but jest—What's here?

(*Enter* Lucy *in a hurry*)

Lucy. O ma'am, here is Sir Anthony Absolute just come home with your aunt.

Lydia. They'll not come here.—Lucy, do you watch. (*Exit* Lucy)

JULIA. Yet I must go. Sir Anthony does not know I am here, and if we meet, he'll detain me, to show me the town. I'll take another opportunity of paying my respects to Mrs. Malaprop, when she shall treat me, as long as she chooses, with her select words so ingeniously misapplied, without being mispronounced.

(Re-enter LUCY*)*

LUCY. O Lud! ma'am, they are both coming upstairs.

LYDIA. Well, I'll not detain you, coz.[17]—Adieu, my dear Julia. I'm sure you are in haste to send to Faulkland.—There, through my room you'll find another staircase.

JULIA. Adieu!   *(Embraces* LYDIA, *and exit)*

LYDIA. Here, my dear Lucy, hide these books. Quick, quick!—Fling *Peregrine Pickle* under the toilet[18]—throw *Roderick Random*[19] into the closet— put *The Innocent Adultery*[20] into *The Whole Duty of Man*—thrust *Lord Aimworth*[21] under the sofa—cram *Ovid* [22] behind the bolster—there—put *The Man of Feeling*[23] into your pocket—so, so—now lay *Mrs. Chapone*[24] in sight, and leave *Fordyce's Sermons*[25] open on the table.

LUCY. O burn it, ma'am! the hair-dresser has torn away[26] as far as "Proper Pride."

[17] **coz** dear friend   [18] **toilet** dressing table   [19] *Roderick Random,* a novel by Smollett   [20] *The Innocent Adultery* translated from the French of Paul Scarron   [21] *Lord Aimworth,* i.e., *The History of Lord Aimworth and the Hon. Charles Hartford, esq.,* a novel in letters   [22] *Ovid* Roman poet; Lydia was doubtless reading a translation of his celebrated poem on *The Art of Love*   [23] *The Man of Feeling* a collection of sentimental character sketches by Henry Mackenzie, 1771   [24] *Mrs Chapone* authoress of a tract attacking the *Letters of Lord Chesterfield to His Son* as teaching immoral conduct. *The Letters* were highly regarded as a guide to proper behavior in good society   [25] *Fordyce's Sermons,* i.e., *Sermons to Young Women,* by Dr. James Fordyce, 1765   [26] **torn away** i.e., to make curl papers

LYDIA. Never mind—open at "Sobriety."—Fling me *Lord Chesterfield's Letters*. Now for 'em. (*Exit* LUCY)

(*Enter* MRS. MALAPROP *and* SIR ANTHONY ABSOLUTE)

MRS. MALAPROP. There, Sir Anthony, there sits the deliberate simpleton who wants to disgrace her family, and lavish herself on a fellow not worth a shilling.

LYDIA. Madam, I thought you once—

MRS. MALAPROP. You thought, miss! I don't know any business you have to think at all—thought does not become a young woman. But the point we would request of you is, that you will promise to forget this fellow—to illiterate him, I say, quite from your memory.

LYDIA. Ah, madam! our memories are independent of our wills. It is not so easy to forget.

MRS. MALAPROP. But I say it is, miss; there is nothing on earth so easy as to forget, if a person chooses to set about it. I'm sure I have as much forgot your poor dear uncle as if he had never existed—and I thought it my duty so to do; and let me tell you, Lydia, these violent memories don't become a young woman.

SIR ANTHONY. Why sure she won't pretend to remember what she's ordered not!—ay, this comes of her reading!

LYDIA. What crime, madam, have I committed, to be treated thus?

MRS. MALAPROP. Now don't attempt to extirpate yourself from the matter; you know I have proof controvertible of it.—But tell me, will you promise to do as you're bid? Will you take a husband of your friends' choosing?

LYDIA. Madam, I must tell you plainly, that had I no preference for any one else, the choice you have made would be my aversion.

MRS. MALAPROP. What business have you, miss, with preference and aversion? They don't become a young woman; and you ought to know, that as both always wear off, 'tis safest in matrimony to begin with a little aversion. I am sure I hated your poor dear uncle before marriage as if he'd been a blackamoor—and yet, miss, you are sensible what a wife I made!—and when it pleased Heaven to release me from him, 'tis unknown what tears I shed! But suppose we were going to give you another choice, will you promise us to give up this Beverley?

LYDIA.   Could I belie my thoughts so far as to give that promise, my actions would certainly as far belie my words.

MRS. MALAPROP.   Take yourself to your room. You are fit company for nothing but your own ill-humours.

LYDIA.   Willingly, ma'am—I cannot change for the worse.   (*Exit*)

MRS. MALAPROP.   There's a little intricate hussy for you!

SIR ANTHONY.   It is not to be wondered at, ma'am, —all this is the natural consequence of teaching girls to read. Had I a thousand daughters, by Heaven! I'd as soon have them taught the black art[27] as their alphabet!

MRS. MALAPROP.   Nay, nay, Sir Anthony, you are an absolute misanthropy.

SIR ANTHONY.   In my way hither, Mrs. Malaprop, I observed your niece's maid coming forth from a circulating library!—She had a book in each hand—they were half-bound volumes, with marbled covers!— From that moment I guessed how full of duty I should see her mistress!

MRS. MALAPROP.   Those are vile places, indeed!

SIR ANTHONY.   Madam, a circulating library in a town is as an evergreen tree of diabolical knowledge! It blossoms through the year!—and depend on it, Mrs. Malaprop, that they who are so fond of handling the leaves, will long for the fruit at last.

[27] **black art** black magic

MRS. MALAPROP. Fie, fie, Sir Anthony, you surely speak laconically.

SIR ANTHONY. Why, Mrs. Malaprop, in moderation now, what would you have a woman know?

MRS. MALAPROP. Observe me, Sir Anthony. I would by no means wish a daughter of mine to be a progeny of learning; I don't think so much learning becomes a young woman; for instance, I would never let her meddle with Greek, or Hebrew, or algebra, or simony, or fluxions, or paradoxes, or such inflammatory branches of learning—neither would it be necessary for her to handle any of your mathematical, astronomical, diabolical instruments.—But, Sir Anthony, I would send her, at nine years old, to a boarding-school, in order to learn a little ingenuity and artifice. Then, sir, she should have a supercilious knowledge in accounts;—and as she grew up, I would have her instructed in geometry, that she might know something of the contagious countries;—but above all, Sir Anthony, she should be mistress of orthodoxy, that she might not mis-spell and mis-pronounce words so shamefully as girls usually do; and likewise that she might reprehend the true meaning of what she is saying. This, Sir Anthony, is what I would have a woman know;—and I don't think there is a superstitious article in it.

SIR ANTHONY. Well, well, Mrs. Malaprop, I will dispute the point no further with you; though I must confess that you are a truly moderate and polite arguer, for almost every third word you say is on my side of the question. But, Mrs. Malaprop, to the more important point in debate—you say you have no objection to my proposal?

MRS. MALAPROP. None, I assure you. I am under no positive engagement with Mr. Acres, and as Lydia is so obstinate against him, perhaps your son may have better success.

SIR ANTHONY. Well, madam, I will write for the

boy directly. He knows not a syllable of this yet, though I have for some time had the proposal in my head. He is at present with his regiment.

MRS. MALAPROP. We have never seen your son, Sir Anthony; but I hope no objection on his side.

SIR ANTHONY. Objection!—let him object if he dare!—No, no, Mrs. Malaprop, Jack knows that the least demur puts me in a frenzy directly. My process was always very simple—in their younger days, 'twas "Jack do this";—if he demurred, I knocked him down —and if he grumbled at that, I always sent him out of the room.

MRS. MALAPROP. Ah, and the properest way, o' my conscience!—nothing is so conciliating to young people as severity.—Well, Sir Anthony, I shall give Mr. Acres his discharge, and prepare Lydia to receive your son's invocations;—and I hope you will represent her to the captain as an object not altogether illegible.

SIR ANTHONY. Madam, I will handle the subject prudently.—Well, I must leave you; and let me beg you, Mrs. Malaprop, to enforce this matter roundly to the girl.—Take my advice—keep a tight hand; if she rejects this proposal, clap her under lock and key; and if you were just to let the servants forget to bring her dinner for three or four days, you can't conceive how she'd come about!   (*Exit*)

MRS. MALAPROP. Well, at any rate, I shall be glad to get her from under my intuition. She has somehow discovered my partiality for Sir Lucius O'Trigger —sure, Lucy can't have betrayed me!—No, the girl is such a simpleton, I should have made her confess it.— (*Calls*) Lucy!—Lucy!—Had she been one of your artificial ones, I should never have trusted her.

(*Enter* LUCY)

LUCY. —Did you call, ma'am?

MRS. MALAPROP. Yes, girl.—Did you see Sir Lucius while you was out?

LUCY. No, indeed, ma'am, not a glimpse of him.

MRS. MALAPROP. You are sure, Lucy, that you never mentioned——

LUCY. Oh, gemini! [28] I'd sooner cut my tongue out.

MRS. MALAPROP. Well, don't let your simplicity[29] be imposed on.

LUCY. No, ma'am.

MRS. MALAPROP. So, come to me presently, and I'll give you another letter to Sir Lucius; but mind, Lucy—if ever you betray what you are entrusted with (unless it be other people's secrets to me), you forfeit my malevolence for ever, and your being a simpleton shall be no excuse for your locality. *(Exit)*

LUCY. Ha! ha! ha!—So, my dear Simplicity, let me give you a little respite.—(*Altering her manner*) Let girls in my station be as fond as they please of appearing expert, and knowing in their trusts; commend me to a mask of silliness, and a pair of sharp eyes for my own interest under it!—Let me see to what account have I turned my simplicity lately.—(*Looks at a paper*) For *abetting Miss Lydia Languish in a design of running away with an ensign: in money, sundry times, twelve pound twelve; gowns, five; hats, ruffles, caps, etc., etc., numberless!—From the said ensign, within this last month, six guineas and a half.*—About a quarter's pay!—Item, *from Mrs. Malaprop, for betraying the young people to her*—when I found matters were likely to be discovered—*two guineas and a black paduasoy.*[30]—Item, *from Mr. Acres, for carrying divers letters*—which I never delivered—*two guineas and a pair of buckles*—Item, *from Sir Lucius O'Trigger, three crowns, two gold pocket-pieces, and a silver snuff-box!*—Well done, Simplicity!—Yet I was forced to make my Hibernian believe that he was corresponding, not with the aunt, but with the niece; for though

[28] gemini jimminy (a mild oath) [29] simplicity unsophistication
[30] *paduasoy* silk dress

not over rich, I found he had too much pride and
delicacy to sacrifice the feelings of a gentleman to the
necessities of his fortune.   (*Exit*)

Act II

Scene I: Captain Absolute's *Lodgings*

(Captain Absolute *and* Fag)

Fag.   Sir, while I was there, Sir Anthony came in:
I told him you had sent me to inquire after his health,
and to know if he was at leisure to see you.

Absolute.   And what did he say, on hearing I was
at Bath?

Fag.   Sir, in my life I never saw an elderly gentleman more astonished! He started back two or three
paces, rapped out a dozen interjectural oaths, and
asked what the devil had brought you here.

Absolute.   Well, sir, and what did you say?

Fag.   Oh, I lied, sir—I forget the precise lie; but
you may depend on't, he got no truth from me. Yet,
with submission, for fear of blunders in future, I
should be glad to fix what *has* brought us to Bath, in
order that we may lie a little consistently. Sir Anthony's
servants were curious, sir, very curious indeed.

Absolute.   You have said nothing to them—?

Fag.   Oh, not a word, sir,—not a word! Mr.
Thomas, indeed, the coachman (whom I take to be the
discreetest of whips)——

Absolute.   'Sdeath!—you rascal! you have not
trusted him!

Fag.   Oh, *no,* sir—no—no—not a syllable, upon

veracity!—He was, indeed, a little inquisitive; but I was sly, sir—devilish sly! My master (said I), honest Thomas (you know, sir, one says honest to one's inferiors), is come to Bath to recruit.—Yes, sir, I said to recruit—and whether for men, money, or constitution, you know, sir, is nothing to him nor any one else.

ABSOLUTE. Well, recruit will do—let it be so.

FAG. Oh, sir, recruit will do surprisingly—indeed, to give the thing an air, I told Thomas that your honour had already enlisted five disbanded chairmen,[1] seven minority waiters,[2] and thirteen billiard-markers.

ABSOLUTE. You blockhead, never say more than is necessary.

FAG. I beg pardon, sir—I beg pardon—but, with submission, a lie is nothing unless one supports it. Sir, whenever I draw on my invention for a good current lie, I always forge indorsements as well as the bill.

ABSOLUTE. Well, take care you don't hurt your credit by offering too much security.—Is Mr. Faulkland returned?

FAG. He is above, sir, changing his dress.

ABSOLUTE. Can you tell whether he has been informed of Sir Anthony's and Miss Melville's arrival?

FAG. I fancy not, sir; he has seen no one since he came in but his gentleman, who was with him at Bristol.—I think, sir, I hear Mr. Faulkland coming down——

ABSOLUTE. Go tell him I am here.

FAG. Yes, sir.—(*Going*) I beg pardon, sir, but should Sir Anthony call, you will do me the favour to remember that we are recruiting, if you please.

ABSOLUTE. Well, well.

FAG. And, in tenderness to my character, if your honour could bring in the chairmen and waiters, I should esteem it as an obligation; for though I never

[1] chairmen who pushed invalids in wheeled chairs   [2] minority waiters unemployed waiters(?)

scruple a lie to serve my master, yet it hurts one's conscience to be found out.   (*Exit*)

ABSOLUTE.   Now for my whimsical friend—if he does not know that his mistress is here, I'll tease him a little before I tell him——

(*Enter* FAULKLAND)

Faulkland, you're welcome to Bath again; you are punctual in your return.

FAULKLAND.   Yes; I had nothing to detain me when I had finished the business I went on. Well, what news since I left you? how stand matters between you and Lydia?

ABSOLUTE.   Faith, much as they were; I have not seen her since our quarrel; however, I expect to be recalled every hour.

FAULKLAND.   Why don't you persuade her to go off with you at once?

ABSOLUTE.   What, and lose two-thirds of her fortune? You forget that, my friend.—No, no, I could have brought her to that long ago.

FAULKLAND.   Nay, then, you trifle too long—if you are sure of her, propose to the aunt in your own character, and write Sir Anthony for his consent.

ABSOLUTE.   Softly, softly; for though I am convinced my little Lydia would elope with me as Ensign Beverley, yet am I by no means certain that she would take me with the impediment of our friends' consent, a regular humdrum wedding, and the reversion[3] of a good fortune on my side; no, no, I must prepare her gradually for the discovery, and make myself necessary to her, before I risk it.—Well, but Faulkland; you'll dine with us to-day at the hotel?

FAULKLAND.   Indeed, I cannot; I am not in spirits to be of such a party.

ABSOLUTE.   By heavens! I shall forswear your com-

[3] reversion eventual inheritance

pany. You are the most teasing, captious, incorrigible lover!—Do love like a man.

FAULKLAND. I own I am unfit for company.

ABSOLUTE. Am not *I* a lover; ay, and a romantic one too? Yet do I carry everywhere with me such a confounded farrago[4] of doubts, fears, hopes, wishes, and all the flimsy furniture of a country miss's brain!

FAULKLAND. Ah! Jack, your heart and soul are not, like mine, fixed immutably on one only object. You throw for a large stake, but losing, you could stake and throw again:—but I have set my sum of happiness on this cast, and not to succeed were to be stripped of all.

ABSOLUTE. But, for heaven's sake! what grounds for apprehension can your whimsical brain conjure up at present?

FAULKLAND. What grounds for apprehension, did you say? Heavens! are there not a thousand! I fear for her spirits—her health—her life.—My absence may fret her; her anxiety for my return, her fears for me, may oppress her gentle temper: and for her health, does not every hour bring me cause to be alarmed? If it rains, some shower may even then have chilled her delicate frame! If the wind be keen, some rude blast may have affected her! The heat of noon, the dews of the evening, may endanger the life of her for whom only I value mine. O! Jack, when delicate and feeling souls are separated, there is not a feature in the sky, not a movement of the elements, not an aspiration of the breeze, but hints some cause for a lover's apprehension!

ABSOLUTE. Ay, but we may choose whether we will take the hint or not.—So then, Faulkland, if you were convinced that Julia were well and in spirits, you would be entirely content?

FAULKLAND. I should be happy beyond measure— I am anxious only for that.

[4] farrago mixture

ABSOLUTE. Then to cure your anxiety at once—Miss Melville is in perfect health, and is at this moment in Bath.

FAULKLAND. Nay, Jack—don't trifle with me.

ABSOLUTE. She is arrived here with my father within this hour.

FAULKLAND. Can you be serious?

ABSOLUTE. I thought you knew Sir Anthony better than to be surprised at a sudden whim of this kind.—Seriously, then, it is as I tell you—upon my honour.

FAULKLAND. My dear friend!—Hollo, Du-Peigne! my hat.—My dear Jack—now nothing on earth can give me a moment's uneasiness.

(Enter FAG*)*

FAG. Sir, Mr. Acres, just arrived, is below.

ABSOLUTE. Stay, Faulkland, this Acres lives within a mile of Sir Anthony, and he shall tell you how your mistress has been ever since you left her. Fag, show the gentleman up.   *(Exit* FAG*)*

FAULKLAND. What, is he much acquainted in the family?

ABSOLUTE. Oh, very intimate: I insist on your not going: besides, his character will divert you.

FAULKLAND. Well, I should like to ask him a few questions.

ABSOLUTE. He is likewise a rival of mine—that is, of my other self's, for he does not think his friend Captain Absolute ever saw the lady in question; and it is ridiculous enough to hear him complain to me of one Beverley, a concealed skulking rival, who——

FAULKLAND. Hush!—he's here.

(Enter ACRES*)*

ACRES. Ha! my dear friend, noble captain, and honest Jack, how do'st thou? just arrived, faith, as you see.—Sir, your humble servant. Warm work on the roads, Jack!—Odds whips and wheels! I've travelled like a comet, with a tail of dust all the way as long as the Mall.

ABSOLUTE. Ah! Bob, you are indeed an eccentric[5] planet, but we know your attraction[6] hither.—Give me leave to introduce Mr. Faulkland to you; Mr. Faulkland, Mr. Acres.

ACRES. Sir, I am most heartily glad to see you: sir, I solicit your connections.—Hey, Jack—what, this is Mr. Faulkland, who——

ABSOLUTE. Ay, Bob, Miss Melville's Mr. Faulkland.

ACRES. Odso! she and your father can be but just arrived before me?—I suppose you have seen them. Ah! Mr. Faulkland, you are indeed a happy man.

FAULKLAND. I have not seen Miss Melville yet, sir; —I hope she enjoyed full health and spirits in Devonshire?

ACRES. Never knew her better in my life, sir,— never better. Odds blushes and blooms! she has been as healthy as the German Spa.

FAULKLAND. Indeed! I did hear that she had been a little indisposed.

ACRES. False, false, sir—only said to vex you: quite the reverse, I assure you.

FAULKLAND. There, Jack, you see she has the advantage of me; I had almost fretted myself ill.

ABSOLUTE. Now are you angry with your mistress for not having been sick?

FAULKLAND. No, no, you misunderstand me: yet surely a little trifling indisposition is not an unnatural consequence of absence from those we love.—Now confess—isn't there something unkind in this violent, robust, unfeeling health?

ABSOLUTE. Oh, it was very unkind of her to be well in your absence, to be sure!

[5] eccentric without a regular orbit   [6] attraction force which attracts

ACRES. Good apartments, Jack.

FAULKLAND. Well, sir, but you were saying that Miss Melville has been so *exceedingly* well—what then she has been merry and gay, I suppose?—Always in spirits—hey?

ACRES. Merry, odds crickets! she has been the belle and spirit of the company wherever she has been—so lively and entertaining! so full of wit and humour!

FAULKLAND. There, Jack, there.—Oh, by my soul! there is an innate levity in woman that nothing can overcome.—What! happy, and I away!

ABSOLUTE. Have done! How foolish this is! just now you were only apprehensive for your mistress' spirits.

FAULKLAND. Why, Jack, have I been the joy and spirit of the company?

ABSOLUTE. No, indeed, you have not.

FAULKLAND. Have I been lively and entertaining?

ABSOLUTE. Oh, upon my word, I acquit you.

FAULKLAND. Have I been full of wit and humour?

ABSOLUTE. No, faith, to do you justice, you have been confoundedly stupid indeed.

ACRES. What's the matter with the gentleman?

ABSOLUTE. He is only expressing his great satisfaction at hearing that Julia has been so well and happy —that's all—hey, Faulkland?

FAULKLAND. Oh! I am rejoiced to hear it—yes, yes, she has a happy disposition!

ACRES. That she has indeed—then she is so accomplished—so sweet a voice—so expert at her harpsichord—such a mistress of flat and sharp,[7] squallante, rumblante, and quiverante![8]—There was this time month—odds minums and crotchets![9] how she did chirrup at Mrs. Piano's concert!

FAULKLAND. There again, what say you to this?

[7] flat and sharp musical terms [8] squallante . . . quiverante burlesque musical terms [9] minims and crochets half-notes and quarter-notes

you see she has been all mirth and song—not a thought of me!

ABSOLUTE. Pho! man, is not music the food of love?

FAULKLAND. Well, well, it may be so.—Pray, Mr. ——, what's his damned name?—Do you remember what songs Miss Melville sung?

ACRES. Not I indeed.

ABSOLUTE. Stay, now, they were some pretty, melancholy, purling-stream airs, I warrant; perhaps you may recollect;—did she sing, *When absent from my soul's delight?*

ACRES. No, that wa'n't it.

ABSOLUTE. Or, *Go, gentle gales!*   (*Sings*)

ACRES. Oh, no! nothing like it. Odds! now I recollect one of them—*My heart's my own, my will is free.*   (*Sings*)

FAULKLAND. Fool! fool that I am! to fix all my happiness on such a trifler! 'Sdeath! to make herself the pipe and ballad-monger of a circle! to soothe her light heart with catches and glees!—What can you say to this, sir?

ABSOLUTE. Why, that I should be glad to hear my mistress had been so merry, *sir*.

FAULKLAND. Nay, nay, nay—I'm not sorry that she has been happy—no, no, I am glad of that—I would not have had her sad or sick—yet surely a sympathetic heart would have shown itself even in the choice of a song—she might have been temperately healthy, and somehow, plaintively gay;—but she has been dancing too, I doubt not!

ACRES. What does the gentleman say about dancing?

ABSOLUTE. He says the lady we speak of dances as well as she sings.

ACRES. Ay, truly, does she—there was at our last race ball [10]——

[10] race ball dance held in connection with a race-meeting

FAULKLAND. Hell and the devil!—There!—there—I told you so! I told you so! Oh! she thrives in my absence!—Dancing! But her whole feelings have been in opposition with mine;—I have been anxious, silent, pensive, sedentary—my days have been hours of care, my nights of watchfulness.[11]—She has been all health! spirit! laugh! song! dance!—Oh! damned, damned levity!

ABSOLUTE. For heaven's sake, Faulkland, don't expose yourself so!—Suppose she has danced, what then?—does not the ceremony of society often oblige——

FAULKLAND. Well, well, I'll contain myself—perhaps as you say—for form sake.—What, Mr. Acres, you were praising Miss Melville's manner of dancing a minuet—hey?

ACRES. Oh, I dare insure her for that—but what I was going to speak of was her country dancing. Odds swimmings! she has such an air with her!

FAULKLAND. Now disappointment on her!—Defend this, Absolute; why don't you defend this?—Country-dances! jigs and reels! am I to blame now? A minuet I could have forgiven—I should not have minded that—I say I should not have regarded a minuet—but country-dances!—Zounds! had she made one in a cotillon—I believe I could have forgiven even that—but to be monkey-led for a night!—to run the gauntlet through a string of amorous palming puppies!—to show paces like a managed filly!—Oh, Jack, there never can be but one man in the world whom a truly modest and delicate woman ought to pair with in a country-dance; and, even then, the rest of the couples should be her great-uncles and aunts!

ABSOLUTE. Ay, to be sure!—grandfathers and grandmothers!

FAULKLAND. If there be but one vicious mind in

[11] watchfulness sleeplessness

the set, 'twill spread like a contagion—the action of their pulse beats to the lascivious movement of the jig—their quivering, warm-breathed sighs impregnate the very air—the atmosphere becomes electrical to love, and each amorous spark darts through every link of the chain!—I must leave you—I own I am somewhat flurried—and that confounded looby has perceived it. (*Going*)

ABSOLUTE. Nay, but stay, Faulkland, and thank Mr. Acres for his good news.

FAULKLAND. Damn his news! (*Exit*)

ABSOLUTE. Ha! ha! ha! poor Faulkland. Five minutes since,[12] "nothing on earth could give him a moment's uneasiness!"

ACRES. The gentleman wa'n't angry at my praising his mistress, was he?

ABSOLUTE. A little jealous, I believe, Bob.

ACRES. You don't say so? Ha! ha! jealous of me—that's a good joke.

ABSOLUTE. There's nothing strange in that, Bob: let me tell you, that sprightly grace and insinuating manner of yours will do some mischief among the girls here.

ACRES. Ah! you joke—ha! ha! mischief—ha! ha! but you know I am not my own property, my dear Lydia has forestalled me. She could never abide me in the country, because I used to dress so badly—but odds frogs and tambours![13] I shan't take matters so here—now ancient madam has no voice in it: I'll make my old clothes know who's master. I shall straightway cashier the hunting-frock, and render my leather breeches incapable. My hair has been in training some time.

ABSOLUTE. Indeed!

ACRES. Ay—and though the side curls are a little restive, my hind-part takes it very kindly.

[12] since ago   [13] frogs and tambours embroidered ornaments

ABSOLUTE. Oh, you'll polish, I doubt not.

ACRES. Absolutely I propose so—then if I can find out this Ensign Beverley, odds triggers and flints! I'll make him know the difference o't.

ABSOLUTE. Spoke like a man! But pray, Bob, I observe you have got an odd kind of a new method of swearing——

ACRES. Ha! ha! you've taken notice of it—'tis genteel, isn't it!—I didn't invent it myself though; but a commander in our militia, a great scholar, I assure you, says that there is no meaning in the common oaths, and that nothing but their antiquity makes them respectable; because, he says, the ancients would never stick to an oath or two, but would say, by Jove! or by Bacchus! or by Mars! or by Venus! or by Pallas, according to the sentiment: so that to swear with propriety, says my little major, the oath should be an echo to the sense;[14] and this we call the *oath referential,* or *sentimental swearing*—ha! ha! ha! 'tis genteel, isn't it?

ABSOLUTE. Very genteel, and very new, indeed!—and I dare say will supplant all other figures of imprecation.

ACRES. Ay, ay, the best terms will grow obsolete. —Damns have had their day.[15]

(*Re-enter* FAG)

FAG. Sir, there is a gentleman below desires to see you.—Shall I show him into the parlour?

ABSOLUTE. Ay—you may.

ACRES. Well, I must be gone——

ABSOLUTE. Stay; who is it, Fag?

FAG. Your father, sir.

ABSOLUTE. You puppy, why didn't you show him up directly? (*Exit* FAG)

---

[14] oath . . . sense a parody of Pope's "the sound must seem an echo to the sense" [15] Damns have had their day compare the proverb, Every *dog* hath his day

ACRES. You have business with Sir Anthony.—I expect a message from Mrs. Malaprop at my lodgings. I have sent also to my dear friend, Sir Lucius O'Trigger. Adieu, Jack! we must meet at night, when you shall give me a dozen bumpers to little Lydia.

ABSOLUTE. That I will with all my heart.—(*Exit* ACRES) Now for a parental lecture—I hope he has heard nothing of the business that brought me here—I wish the gout had held him fast in Devonshire, with all my soul!

(*Enter* SIR ANTHONY ABSOLUTE)

Sir, I am delighted to see you here and looking so well! your sudden arrival at Bath made me apprehensive for your health.

SIR ANTHONY. Very apprehensive, I dare say, Jack. —What, you are recruiting here, hey?

ABSOLUTE. Yes, sir, I am on duty.

SIR ANTHONY. Well, Jack, I am glad to see you, though I did not expect it, for I was going to write to you on a little matter of business.—Jack, I have been considering that I grow old and infirm, and shall probably not trouble you long.

ABSOLUTE. Pardon, sir, I never saw you look more strong and hearty; and I pray frequently that you may continue so.

SIR ANTHONY. I hope your prayers may be heard, with all my heart. Well, then, Jack, I have been considering that I am so strong and hearty I may continue to plague you a long time. Now, Jack, I am sensible that the income of your commission, and what I have hitherto allowed you, is but a small pittance for a lad of your spirit.

ABSOLUTE. Sir, you are very good.

SIR ANTHONY. And it is my wish, while yet I live, to have my boy make some figure in the world. I have resolved, therefore, to fix you at once in a noble independence.

ABSOLUTE.   Sir, your kindness overpowers me—such generosity makes the gratitude of reason more lively than the sensations even of filial affection.

SIR ANTHONY.   I am glad you are so sensible of my attention—and you shall be master of a large estate in a few weeks.

ABSOLUTE.   Let my future life, sir, speak my gratitude; I cannot express the sense I have of your munificence.—Yet, sir, I presume you would not wish me to quit the army?

SIR ANTHONY.   Oh, that shall be as your wife chooses.

ABSOLUTE.   My wife, sir!

SIR ANTHONY.   Ay, ay, settle that between you—settle that between you.

ABSOLUTE.   A *wife*, sir, did you say?

SIR ANTHONY.   Ay, a wife—why, did not I mention her before?

ABSOLUTE.   Not a word of her, sir.

SIR ANTHONY.   Odd so!—I mus'n't forget *her* though.—Yes, Jack, the independence I was talking of is by marriage—the fortune is saddled with a wife—but I suppose that makes no difference.

ABSOLUTE.   Sir! sir!—you amaze me!

SIR ANTHONY.   Why, what the devil's the matter with the fool? Just now you were all gratitude and duty.

ABSOLUTE.   I was, sir—you talked to me of independence and a fortune, but not a word of a wife.

SIR ANTHONY.   Why—what difference does that make? Odds life, sir! if you have the estate, you must take it with the live stock on it, as it stands.

ABSOLUTE.   If my happiness is to be the price, I must beg leave to decline the purchase.—Pray, sir, who is the lady?

SIR ANTHONY. What's that to you, sir?—Come, give me your promise to love, and to marry her directly.

ABSOLUTE. Sure, sir, this is not very reasonable, to summon my affections for a lady I know nothing of!

SIR ANTHONY. I am sure, sir, 'tis more unreasonable in you to *object* to a lady you know nothing of.

ABSOLUTE. Then, sir, I must tell you plainly that my inclinations are fixed on another—my heart is engaged to an angel.

SIR ANTHONY. Then pray let it send an excuse. It is very sorry—but business prevents its waiting on her.

ABSOLUTE. But my vows are pledged to her.

SIR ANTHONY. Let her foreclose, Jack; let her foreclose; they are not worth redeeming; besides, you have the angel's vows in exchange, I suppose; so there can be no loss there.

ABSOLUTE. You must excuse me, sir, if I tell you, once for all, that in this point I cannot obey you.

SIR ANTHONY. Hark'ee, Jack;—I have heard you for some time with patience—I have been cool—quite cool; but take care—you know I am compliance itself —when I am not thwarted;—no one more easily led —when I have my own way;—but don't put me in a frenzy.

ABSOLUTE. Sir, I must repeat—in this I cannot obey you.

SIR ANTHONY. Now damn me! if ever I call you Jack again while I live!

ABSOLUTE. Nay, sir, but hear me.

SIR ANTHONY. Sir, I won't hear a word—not a word! not one word! so give me your promise by a nod—and I'll tell you what, Jack—I mean, you dog —if you don't, by——

ABSOLUTE. What, sir, promise to link myself to some mass of ugliness! to——

SIR ANTHONY. Zounds! sirrah! the lady shall be as ugly as I choose: she shall have a hump on each shoulder; she shall be as crooked as the crescent; her one eye shall roll like the bull's in Cox's Museum,[16] she shall have a skin like a mummy, and the beard of a Jew—she shall be all this, sirrah!—yet I will make you ogle her all day, and sit up all night to write sonnets on her beauty.

ABSOLUTE. This is reason and moderation indeed!

SIR ANTHONY. None of your sneering, puppy! no grinning, jackanapes!

ABSOLUTE. Indeed, sir, I never was in a worse humour for mirth in my life.

SIR ANTHONY. 'Tis false, sir. I know you are laughing in your sleeve; I know you'll grin when I am gone, sirrah!

ABSOLUTE. Sir, I hope I know my duty better.

SIR ANTHONY. None of your passion, sir! none of your violence, if you please!—It won't do with me, I promise you.

ABSOLUTE. Indeed, sir, I never was cooler in my life.

SIR ANTHONY. 'Tis a confounded lie!—I know you are in a passion in your heart; I know you are, you hypocritical young dog! but it won't do.

ABSOLUTE. Nay, sir, upon my word——

SIR ANTHONY. So you will fly out! can't you be cool like me? What the devil good can passion do?—Passion is of no service, you impudent, insolent, overbearing reprobate!—There, you sneer again! don't provoke me!—but you rely upon the mildness of my temper—you do, you dog! you play upon the meekness of my disposition!—Yet take care—the patience of a saint may be overcome at last!—but mark! I give you six hours and a half to consider of this: if you then agree, without any condition, to do everything on

[16] Cox's Museum an exhibition of waxworks and curiosities

earth that I choose, why—confound you! I may in time forgive you.—If not, zounds! don't enter the same hemisphere with me! don't dare to breathe the same air, or use the same light with me; but get an atmosphere and sun of your own! I'll strip you of your commission; I'll lodge a five-and-threepence in the hands of trustees,[17] and you shall live on the interest.—I'll disown you, I'll disinherit you, I'll unget you! and damn me! if ever I call you Jack again!

(*Exit* Sir Anthony)

Absolute. Mild, gentle, considerate father—I kiss your hands!—What a tender method of giving his opinion in these matters Sir Anthony has! I dare not trust him with the truth.—I wonder what old wealthy hag it is that he wants to bestow on me!—Yet he married himself for love! and was in his youth a bold intriguer, and a gay companion!

(*Re-enter* Fag)

Fag. Assuredly, sir, our father is wrath to a degree; he comes down stairs eight or ten steps at a time— muttering, growling, and thumping the banisters all the way: I and the cook's dog stand bowing at the door—rap! he gives me a stroke on the head with his cane; bids me carry that to my master; then kicking the poor turnspit into the area, damns us all, for a puppy triumvirate!—Upon my credit, sir, were I in your place, and found my father such very bad company, I should certainly drop his acquaintance.

Absolute. Cease your impertinence, sir, at present.—Did you come in for nothing more?—Stand out of the way! (*Pushes him aside, and exit*)

Fag. So! Sir Anthony trims[18] my master; he is afraid to reply to his father—then vents his spleen on poor Fag!—When one is vexed by one person, to

[17] lodge . . . trustees "cut you off with a dollar" [18] trims scolds

revenge one's self on another, who happens to come in the way, is the vilest injustice! Ah! it shows the worst temper—the basest——

(*Enter* BOY)

BOY.   Mr. Fag! Mr. Fag! your master calls you.

FAG.   Well, you little dirty puppy, you need not bawl so!—The meanest disposition! the——

BOY.   Quick, quick, Mr. Fag!

FAG.   Quick! quick! you impudent jackanapes! am I to be commanded by you too? you little, impertinent, insolent, kitchen-bred——

(*Exit kicking and beating him*)

SCENE II: *The North Parade*[1]

(*Enter* LUCY)

LUCY.   So—I shall have another rival to add to my mistress's list—Captain Absolute. However, I shall not enter his name till my purse has received notice in form. Poor Acres is dismissed!—Well, I have done him a last friendly office, in letting him know that Beverley was here before him.—Sir Lucius is generally more punctual, when he expects to hear from his *dear Dalia,* as he calls her: I wonder he's not here!—I have a little scruple of conscience from this deceit; though I should not be paid so well, if my hero knew that Delia was near fifty, and her own mistress.

(*Enter* SIR LUCIUS O'TRIGGER)

SIR LUCIUS.   Ha! my little ambassadress—upon my conscience, I have been looking for you; I have been on the South Parade this half hour.

LUCY.   (*Speaking simply*[2]) O gemini! and I have been waiting for your lordship here on the North.

[1] *The North Parade* fashionable promenade in Bath   [2] *simply* ignorantly

SIR LUCIUS. Faith!—may be that was the reason we did not meet; and it is very comical too, how you could go out and I not see you—for I was only taking a nap at the Parade Coffee-house, and I chose the *window* on purpose that I might not miss you.

LUCY. My stars! Now I'd wager a sixpence I went by while you were asleep.

SIR LUCIUS. Sure enough it must have been so— and I never dreamt it was so late, till I waked. Well, but my little girl, have you got nothing for me?

LUCY. Yes, but I have—I've got a letter for you in my pocket.

SIR LUCIUS. O faith! I guessed you weren't come empty-handed—Well—let me see what the dear creature says.

LUCY. There, Sir Lucius. (*Gives him a letter*)

SIR LUCIUS. (*Reads*) *Sir—there is often a sudden incentive impulse in love, that has a greater induction than years of domestic combination: such was the commotion I felt at the first superfluous view of Sir Lucius O'Trigger.*—Very pretty, upon my word. *Female punctuation forbids me to say more; yet let me add, that it will give me joy infallible to find Sir Lucius worthy the last criterion of my affections.*
                                                    DELIA.

Upon my conscience! Lucy, your lady is a great mistress of language. Faith, she's quite the queen of the dictionary!—for the devil a word dare refuse coming at her call—though one would think it was quite out of hearing.

LUCY. Ay, sir, a lady of her experience——

SIR LUCIUS. Experience! what, at seventeen?

LUCY. O true, sir—but then she reads so—my stars! how she will read off-hand!

SIR LUCIUS. Faith, she must be very deep read to write this way—though she is rather an arbitrary writer too—for here are a great many poor words pressed [3] into the service of this note, that would get their *habeas corpus* [4] from any court in Christendom.

LUCY.   Ah! Sir Lucius, if you were to hear how she talks of you!

SIR LUCIUS.   Oh, tell her I'll make her the best husband in the world, and Lady O'Trigger into the bargain!—But we must get the old gentlewoman's consent—and do everything fairly.

LUCY.   Nay, Sir Lucius, I thought you wa'n't rich enough to be so nice.

SIR LUCIUS.   Upon my word, young woman, you have hit it:—I am so poor, that I can't afford to do a dirty action.—If I did not want money, I'd steal your mistress and her fortune with a great deal of pleasure. —However, my pretty girl (*Give her money*), here's a little something to buy you a ribbon; and meet me in the evening, and I'll give you an answer to this. So, hussy, take a kiss beforehand to put you in mind.

(*Kisses her*)

LUCY.   O Lud! [5] Sir Lucius—I never seed such a genman! My lady won't like you if you're so impudent.

SIR LUCIUS.   Faith she will, Lucy!—That same— pho! what's the name of it?—modesty!—is a quality in a lover more praised by the women than liked; so, if your mistress asks you whether Sir Lucius ever gave you a kiss, tell her fifty—my dear.

LUCY.   What, would you have me tell a lie?

SIR LUCIUS.   Ah, then, you baggage! I'll make it a truth presently.

LUCY.   For shame now! here is some one coming.

SIR LUCIUS.   Oh, faith, I'll quiet your conscience!

([*Sees* FAG]. *Exit humming a tune*)

(*Enter* FAG)

[3] **pressed** drafted   [4] *habeas corpus* a legal process by which a person is delivered from illegal confinement   [5] **Lud** Lord

FAG. So, so, ma'am! I humbly beg pardon.

LUCY. O Lud! now, Mr. Fag, you flurry one so.

FAG. Come, come, Lucy, here's no one by—so a little less simplicity, with a grain or two more sincerity, if you please.—You play false with us, madam.—I saw you give the baronet a letter.—My master shall know this—and if he don't call him out,[6] I will.

LUCY. Ha! ha! ha! you gentlemen's gentlemen are so hasty. That letter was from Mrs. Malaprop, simpleton.—She is taken with Sir Lucius's address.[7]

FAG. How! what tastes some people have!—Why, I suppose I have walked by her window a hundred times.—But what says our young lady? any message to my master?

LUCY. Sad news, Mr. Fag.—A worse rival than Acres! Sir Anthony Absolute has proposed his son.

FAG. What, Captain Absolute?

LUCY. Even so—I overheard it all.

FAG. Ha! ha! ha! very good, faith.—Good-bye, Lucy, I must away with this news.

LUCY. Well, you may laugh—but it is true, I assure you.—(*Going*) But, Mr. Fag, tell your master not to be cast down by this.

FAG. Oh, he'll be so disconsolate!

LUCY. And charge him not to think of quarrelling with young Absolute.

FAG. Never fear! never fear!

LUCY. Be sure—bid him keep up his spirits.

FAG. We will—we will.   (*Exeunt severally*)

[6] call him out challenge him to a duel [7] address behavior, manners

Act III

Scene I: *The North Parade*

(*Enter* CAPTAIN ABSOLUTE)

ABSOLUTE.   'Tis just as Fag told me, indeed. Whimsical enough, faith. My father wants to force me to marry the very girl I am plotting to run away with! He must not know of my connection with her yet awhile. He has too summary a method of proceeding in these matters. However, I'll read my recantation instantly. My conversion is something sudden, indeed —but I can assure him it is very *sincere*. So, so—here he comes. He looks plaguy gruff.   (*Steps aside*)

(*Enter* SIR ANTHONY ABSOLUTE)

SIR ANTHONY.   No—I'll die sooner than forgive him. Die, did I say? I'll live these fifty years to plague him. At our last meeting, his impudence had almost put me out of temper. An obstinate, passionate, self-willed boy! Who can he take after? This is my return for getting him before all his brothers and sisters!— for putting him, at twelve years old, into a marching regiment, and allowing him fifty pounds a year, besides his pay, ever since! But I have done with him; he's anybody's son for me. I never will see him more, never—never—never—never.

ABSOLUTE.   (*Aside, coming forward*) Now for a penitential face.

SIR ANTHONY.   Fellow, get out of my way.

ABSOLUTE.   Sir, you see a penitent before you.

SIR ANTHONY.   I see an impudent scoundrel before me.

ABSOLUTE. A sincere penitent. I am come, sir, to acknowledge my error, and to submit entirely to your will.

SIR ANTHONY. What's that?

ABSOLUTE. I have been revolving, and reflecting, and considering on your past goodness, and kindness, and condescension to me.

SIR ANTHONY. Well, sir?

ABSOLUTE. I have been likewise weighing and balancing what you were pleased to mention concerning duty, and obedience, and authority.

SIR ANTHONY. Well, puppy?

ABSOLUTE. Why, then, sir, the result of my reflections is—a resolution to sacrifice every inclination of my own to your satisfaction.

SIR ANTHONY. Why now you talk sense—absolute sense.—I never heard anything more sensible in my life. Confound you! you shall be Jack again.

ABSOLUTE. I am happy in the appellation.

SIR ANTHONY. Why, then, Jack, my dear Jack, I will now inform you who the lady really is. Nothing but your passion and violence, you silly fellow, prevented my telling you at first. Prepare, Jack, for wonder and rapture—prepare. What think you of Miss Lydia Languish?

ABSOLUTE. Languish! What, the Languishes of Worcestershire?

SIR ANTHONY. Worcestershire! no. Did you ever meet Mrs. Malaprop and her niece, Miss Languish, who came into our country just before you were last ordered to your regiment?

ABSOLUTE. Malaprop! Languish! I don't remember ever to have heard the names before. Yet stay—I think I do recollect something. Languish! Languish! She squints, don't she? A little red-haired girl?

SIR ANTHONY. Squints! A red-haired girl! Zounds! no.

ABSOLUTE.   Then I must have forgot; it can't be the same person.

SIR ANTHONY.   Jack! Jack! what think you of blooming, love-breathing seventeen?

ABSOLUTE.   As to that, sir, I am quite indifferent. If I can please you in the matter, 'tis all I desire.

SIR ANTHONY.   Nay, but, Jack, such eyes! such eyes! so innocently wild! so bashfully irresolute! not a glance but speaks and kindles some thought of love! Then, Jack, her cheeks! her cheeks, Jack! so deeply blushing at the insinuations of her tell-tale eyes! Then, Jack, her lips! O, Jack, lips smiling at their own discretion; and if not smiling, more sweetly pouting; more lovely in sullenness.

ABSOLUTE.   That's she, indeed. Well done, old gentleman.   (*Aside*)

SIR ANTHONY.   Then, Jack, her neck! O Jack! Jack!

ABSOLUTE.   And which is to be mine, sir; the niece or the aunt?

SIR ANTHONY.   Why, you unfeeling, insensible puppy, I despise you! When I was of your age, such a description would have made me fly like a rocket! The aunt, indeed! Odds life! when I ran away with your mother, I would not have touched anything old or ugly to gain an empire.

ABSOLUTE.   Not to please your father, sir?

SIR ANTHONY.   To please my father! zounds! not to please—Oh, my father—odd so!—yes—yes; if my father indeed had desired—that's quite another matter. Though he wa'n't the indulgent father that I am, Jack.

ABSOLUTE.   I dare say not, sir.

SIR ANTHONY.   But, Jack, you are not sorry to find your mistress is so beautiful?

ABSOLUTE.   Sir, I repeat it—if I please you in this affair, 'tis all I desire. Not that I think a woman the worse for being handsome; but, sir, if you please to recollect, you before hinted something about a hump or two, one eye, and a few more graces of that kind—now, without being very nice, I own I should rather choose a wife of mine to have the usual number of limbs, and a limited quantity of back: and though one eye may be very agreeable, yet as the prejudice has always run in favour of two, I would not wish to affect a singularity in that article.

SIR ANTHONY. What a phlegmatic sot it is! Why, sirrah, you're an anchorite![1]—a vile, insensible stock.[2] You a soldier!—you're a walking block, fit only to dust the company's regimentals on! Odds life! I have a great mind to marry the girl myself!

ABSOLUTE. I am entirely at your disposal, sir: if you should think of addressing Miss Languish yourself, I suppose you would have me marry the aunt; or if you should change your mind, and take the old lady—'tis the same to me—I'll marry the niece.

SIR ANTHONY. Upon my word, Jack, thou'rt either a very great hypocrite, or—but, come, I know your indifference on such a subject must be all a lie—I'm sure it must—come, now—damn your demure face! —come, confess, Jack—you have been lying, ha'n't you? You have been playing the hypocrite, hey!—I'll never forgive you, if you ha'n't been lying and playing the hypocrite.

ABSOLUTE. I'm sorry, sir, that the respect and duty which I bear to you should be so mistaken.

SIR ANTHONY. Hang your respect and duty! But come along with me, I'll write a note to Mrs. Malaprop, and you shall visit the lady directly. Her eyes shall be the Promethean torch[3] to you—come along, I'll never forgive you, if you don't come back stark mad with rapture and impatience—if you don't, egad, I will marry the girl myself!   (*Exeunt*)

[1] anchorite hermit   [2] stock block of wood   [3] Promethean torch enkindling spark

Scene II: *Julia's Dressing-Room*

(Faulkland, *alone*)

Faulkland.   They told me Julia would return directly; I wonder she is not yet come! How mean does this captious, unsatisfied temper of mine appear to my cooler judgment! Yet I know not that I indulge it in any other point: but on this one subject, and to this one subject, whom I think I love beyond my life, I am ever ungenerously fretful and madly capricious! I am conscious of it—yet I cannot correct myself! What tender honest joy sparkled in her eyes when we met! how delicate was the warmth of her expressions! I was ashamed to appear less happy—though I had come resolved to wear a face of coolness and upbraiding. Sir Anthony's presence prevented my proposed expostulations; yet I must be satisfied that she has not been so very happy in my absence.—She is coming! Yes!—I know the nimbleness of her tread, when she thinks her impatient Faulkland counts the moments of her stay.

(*Enter* Julia)

Julia.   I had not hoped to see you again so soon.

Faulkland.   Could I, Julia, be contented with my first welcome—restrained as we were by the presence of a third person?

Julia.   O Faulkland, when your kindness can make me thus happy, let me not think that I discovered something of coldness in your first salutation.

Faulkland.   'Twas but your fancy, Julia. I *was* rejoiced to see you—to see you in such health. Sure I had no cause for coldness?

Julia.   Nay, then, I see you have taken something ill. You must not conceal from me what it is.

Faulkland.   Well, then—shall I own to you that

my joy at hearing of your health and arrival here, by your neighbour Acres, was somewhat dampened by his dwelling much on the high spirits you had enjoyed in Devonshire—on your mirth—your singing—dancing, and I know not what! For such is my temper, Julia, that I should regard every mirthful moment in your absence as a treason to constancy. The mutual tear that steals down the cheek of parting lovers is a compact, that no smile shall live there till they meet again.

JULIA. Must I never cease to tax my Faulkland with this teasing minute caprice? Can the idle reports of a silly boor weigh in your breast against my tried affection?

FAULKLAND. They have no weight with me, Julia: No, no—I am happy if you have been so—yet only say, that you did not sing with *mirth*—say that you thought of Faulkland in the dance.

JULIA. I never can be happy in your absence. If I wear a countenance of content, it is to show that my mind holds no doubt of my Faulkland's truth. If I seemed sad, it were to make malice triumph and say, that I fixed my heart on one, who left me to lament his roving, and my own credulity. Believe me, Faulkland, I mean not to upbraid you when I say that I have often dressed sorrow in smiles, lest my friends should guess whose unkindness had caused my tears.

FAULKLAND. You were ever all goodness to me. Oh, I am a brute, when I but admit a doubt of your true constancy!

JULIA. If ever without such cause from you, as I will not suppose possible, you find my affections veering but a point, may I become a proverbial scoff for levity and base ingratitude.

FAULKLAND. Ah! Julia, that last word is grating to me. I would I had no title to your gratitude! Search your heart, Julia; perhaps what you have mistaken for love, is but the warm effusion of a too thankful heart.

JULIA.   For what quality must I love you?

FAULKLAND.   For no quality! To regard me for any quality of mind or understanding, were only to esteem me. And for person—I have often wished myself deformed, to be convinced that I owe no obligation there for any part of your affection.

JULIA.   Where nature has bestowed a show of nice attention in the features of a man, he should laugh at it as misplaced. I have seen men, who in this vain article, perhaps, might rank above you; but my heart has never asked my eyes if it were so or not.

FAULKLAND.   Now this is not well from you, Julia— I despise person[1] in a man—yet if you loved me as I wish, though I were an Æthiop, you'd think none so fair.

JULIA.   I see you are determined to be unkind! The contract which my poor father bound us in gives you more than a lover's privilege.

FAULKLAND.   Again, Julia, you raise ideas that feed and justify my doubts. I would not have been more free—no—I am proud of my restraint. Yet—yet—perhaps your high respect alone for this solemn compact has fettered your inclinations, which else had made a worthier choice. How shall I be sure, had you remained unbound in thought and promise, that I should still have been the object of your persevering love?

JULIA.   Then try me now. Let us be free as strangers as to what is past: my heart will not feel more liberty!

FAULKLAND.   There now! so hasty, Julia! so anxious to be free! If your love for me were fixed and ardent, you would not loose your hold, even though I wished it!

JULIA.   Oh! you torture me to the heart! I cannot bear it.

[1] person i.e., concern for mere appearance, vanity

FAULKLAND. I do not mean to distress you. If I loved you less I should never give you an uneasy moment. But hear me. All my fretful doubts arise from this. Women are not used to weigh and separate the motives of their affections: the cold dictates of prudence, gratitude, or filial duty, may sometimes be mistaken for the pleadings of the heart. I would not boast —yet let me say, that I have neither age, person, or character, to found dislike on; my fortune such as few ladies could be charged with indiscretion in the match. O Julia! when love receives such countenance from prudence, nice minds will be suspicious of its birth.

JULIA. I know not whither your insinuations would tend:—but as they seem pressing to insult me, I will spare you the regret of having done so.—I have given you no cause for this! (*Exit in tears*)

FAULKLAND. In tears! Stay, Julia: stay but for a moment.—The door is fastened!—Julia!—my soul— but for one moment!—I hear her sobbing!—'Sdeath! what a brute am I to use her thus! Yet stay! Ay—she is coming now:—how little resolution there is in a woman!—how a few soft words can turn them!—No, faith!—she is *not* coming either.—Why, Julia—my love—say but that you forgive me—come but to tell me that—now this is being too resentful. Stay! she *is* coming too—I thought she would—no steadiness in anything: her going away must have been a mere trick then—she sha'n't see that I was hurt by it—I'll affect indifference—(*Hums a tune; then listens*) No— zounds! she's *not* coming!—nor don't intend it, I suppose.—This is not steadiness, but obstinacy! Yet I deserve it.—What, after so long an absence to quarrel with her tenderness!—'twas barbarous and unmanly! —I should be ashamed to see her now.—I'll wait till her just resentment is abated—and when I distress her so again, may I lose her for ever! and be linked instead to some antique virago,[2] whose gnawing passions, and long hoarded spleen,[3] shall make me curse my folly half the day and all the night.   (*Exit*)

SCENE III: MRS. MALAPROP's *Lodgings*

(MRS. MALAPROP, *with a letter in her hand, and* CAPTAIN ABSOLUTE)

MRS. MALAPROP. Your being Sir Anthony's son, captain, would itself be a sufficient accommodation; but from the ingenuity of your appearance, I am convinced you deserve the character here given of you.

ABSOLUTE. Permit me to say, madam, that as I never yet have had the pleasure of seeing Miss Languish, my principal inducement in this affair at present is the honour of being allied to Mrs. Malaprop, of whose intellectual accomplishments, elegant manners, and unaffected learning, no tongue is silent.

MRS. MALAPROP. Sir, you do me infinite honour! I beg, captain, you'll be seated.—(*They sit*) Ah! few gentlemen, now-a-days, know how to value the ineffectual qualities in a woman! Few think how a little knowledge becomes a gentlewoman. Men have no sense now but for the worthless flower of beauty!

ABSOLUTE. It is but too true, indeed, ma'am;—yet I fear our ladies should share the blame—they think our admiration of beauty so great, that knowledge in them would be superfluous. Thus, like garden-trees, they seldom show fruit, till time has robbed them of more specious blossom.—Few, like Mrs. Malaprop and the orange-tree, are rich in both at once!

MRS. MALAPROP. Sir, you overpower me with good-breeding.—He is the very pineapple of politeness!— You are not ignorant, captain, that this giddy girl has somehow contrived to fix her affections on a beggarly,

[2] **virago** turbulent woman   [3] **spleen** ill humor

strolling, eavesdropping ensign, whom none of us have seen, and nobody knows anything of.

ABSOLUTE. Oh, I have heard the silly affair before. —I'm not at all prejudiced against her on that account.

MRS. MALAPROP. You are very good and very considerate, captain. I am sure I have done everything in my power since I exploded the affair; long ago I laid my positive conjunctions on her, never to think on the fellow again;—I have since laid Sir Anthony's preposition before her; but, I am sorry to say, she seems resolved to decline every particle that I enjoin her.

ABSOLUTE. It must be very distressing, indeed, ma'am.

MRS. MALAPROP. Oh! it gives me the hydrostatics to such a degree.—I thought she had persisted from corresponding with him; but, behold, this very day, I have interceded another letter from the fellow; I believe I have it in my pocket.

ABSOLUTE. Oh, the devil! my last note. (*Aside*)

MRS. MALAPROP. Ay, here it is.

ABSOLUTE. Ay, my note indeed! Oh, the little traitress Lucy. (*Aside*)

MRS. MALAPROP. There, perhaps you may know the writing. (*Gives him the letter*)

ABSOLUTE. I think I have seen the hand before— yes, I certainly must have seen this hand before——

MRS. MALAPROP. Nay, but read it, captain.

ABSOLUTE. (*Reads*) *My soul's idol, my adored Lydia!*—Very tender, indeed!

MRS. MALAPROP. Tender, ay, and profane too, o' my conscience.

ABSOLUTE. (*Reads*) *I am excessively alarmed at the intelligence you send me, the more so as my new rival——*

MRS. MALAPROP. That's you, sir.

ABSOLUTE. (*Reads*) *Has universally the character*

of being an accomplished gentleman and a man of honour.—Well, that's handsome enough.

MRS. MALAPROP.   Oh, the fellow has some design in writing so.

ABSOLUTE.   That he had, I'll answer for him, ma'am.

MRS. MALAPROP.   But go on, sir—you'll see presently.

ABSOLUTE.   (*Reads*) *As for the old weather-beaten she-dragon who guards you.*—Who can he mean by that?

MRS. MALAPROP.   Me, sir!—me!—he means me!—There—what do you think now?—but go on a little further.

ABSOLUTE.   Impudent scoundrel!—(*Reads*) *it shall go hard but I will elude her vigilance, as I am told that the same ridiculous vanity, which makes her dress up her coarse features, and deck her dull chat with hard words which she don't understand*——

MRS. MALAPROP.   There, sir, an attack upon my language! what do you think of that?—an aspersion upon my parts of speech! was ever such a brute! Sure, if I reprehend any thing in this world it is the use of my oracular tongue, and a nice derangement of epitaphs!

ABSOLUTE.   He deserves to be hanged and quartered! let me see—(*Reads*) *same ridiculous vanity*——

MRS. MALAPROP.   You need not read it again, sir.

ABSOLUTE.   I beg pardon, ma'am.—(*Reads*) *does also lay her open to the grossest deceptions from flattery and pretended admiration*—an impudent coxcomb!—*so that I have a scheme to see you shortly with the old harridan's consent, and even to make her a go-between in our interview.*—Was ever such assurance!

MRS. MALAPROP.   Did you ever hear anything like it?—he'll elude my vigilance, will he?—Yes, yes! ha! ha! he's very likely to enter these doors;—we'll try who can plot best!

ABSOLUTE. So we will, ma'am—so we will! Ha! ha! ha! a conceited puppy, ha! ha! ha!—Well, but, Mrs. Malaprop, as the girl seems so infatuated by this fellow, suppose you were to wink at her corresponding with him for a little time—let her even plot an elopement with him—then do you connive at her escape—while I, just in the nick, will have the fellow laid by the heels, and fairly contrive to carry her off in his stead.

MRS. MALAPROP. I am delighted with the scheme; never was anything better perpetrated!

ABSOLUTE. But, pray, could not I see the lady for a few minutes now?—I should like to try her temper a little.

MRS. MALAPROP. Why, I don't know—I doubt[4] she is not prepared for a visit of this kind. There is a decorum in these matters.

ABSOLUTE. O Lord! she won't mind me—only tell her Beverley——

MRS. MALAPROP. Sir!

ABSOLUTE. Gently, good tongue. (*Aside*)

MRS. MALAPROP. What did you say of Beverley?

ABSOLUTE. Oh, I was going to propose that you should tell her, by way of jest, that it was Beverley who was below; she'd come down fast enough then—ha! ha! ha!

MRS. MALAPROP. 'Twould be a trick she well deserves; besides, you know the fellow tells her he'll get my consent to see her—ha! ha! Let him if he can, I say again. Lydia, come down here!—(*Calling*) He'll make me a go-between in their interviews!—ha! ha! ha! Come down, I say, Lydia! I don't wonder at your laughing, ha! ha! ha! his impudence is truly ridiculous.

ABSOLUTE. 'Tis very ridiculous, upon my soul, ma'am, ha! ha! ha!

MRS. MALAPROP. The little hussy won't hear. Well,

⁴ doubt fear

I'll go and tell her at once who it is—she shall know that Captain Absolute is come to wait on her. And I'll make her behave as becomes a young woman.

ABSOLUTE. As you please, madam.

MRS. MALAPROP. For the present, captain, your servant. Ah! you've not done laughing yet, I see— elude my vigilance; yes, yes; ha! ha! ha! (*Exit*)

ABSOLUTE. Ha! ha! ha! one would think now that I might throw off all disguise at once, and seize my prize with security; but such is Lydia's caprice, that to undeceive were probably to lose her. I'll see whether she knows me.

(*Walks aside, and seems engaged in looking at the pictures*)

(*Enter* LYDIA)

LYDIA. What a scene am I now to go through! surely nothing can be more dreadful than to be obliged to listen to the loathsome addresses of a stranger to one's heart. I have heard of girls persecuted as I am, who have appealed in behalf of their favoured lover to the generosity of his rival; suppose I were to try it— there stands the hated rival—an officer too;—but oh, how unlike my Beverley! I wonder he don't begin— truly he seems a very negligent wooer!—quite at his ease, upon my word! I'll speak first—Mr. Absolute.

ABSOLUTE. Ma'am. (*Turns round*)

LYDIA. O heavens! Beverley!

ABSOLUTE. Hush;—hush, my life! softly! be not surprised!

LYDIA. I am so astonished; and so terrified and so overjoyed!—for Heaven's sake! how came you here?

ABSOLUTE. Briefly, I have deceived your aunt—I was informed that my new rival was to visit here this evening, and contriving to have him kept away, have passed myself on her for Captain Absolute.

LYDIA.   O charming! And she really takes you for young Absolute.

ABSOLUTE.   Oh, she's convinced of it.

LYDIA.   Ha! Ha! ha! I can't forbear laughing to think how her sagacity is overreached!

ABSOLUTE.   But we trifle with our precious moments —such another opportunity may not occur; then let me conjure my kind, my condescending angel, to fix the time when I may rescue her from undeserving persecution, and with a licensed warmth plead for my reward.

LYDIA.   Will you then, Beverley, consent to forfeit that portion of my paltry wealth?—that burden on the wings of love?

ABSOLUTE.   Oh, come to me—rich only thus—in loveliness! Bring no portion to me but thy love—'twill be generous in you, Lydia,—for well you know it is the only dower your poor Beverley can repay.

LYDIA.   How persuasive are his words!—how charming will poverty be with him!   (*Aside*)

ABSOLUTE.   Ah! my soul, what a life will we then live! Love shall be our idol and support! we will worship him with a monastic strictness; abjuring all worldly toys, to centre every thought and action there. Proud of calamity, we will enjoy the wreck of wealth; while the surrounding gloom of adversity shall make the flame of our pure love show doubly bright. By Heavens! I would fling all goods of fortune from me with a prodigal hand, to enjoy the scene where I might clasp my Lydia to my bosom, and say, the world affords no smile to me but here—(*Embracing her*) If she holds out now, the devil is in it!   (*Aside*)

LYDIA.   Now could I fly with him to the antipodes! [5] but my persecution is not yet come to a crisis.
(*Aside*)

---

[5] antipodes the "ends of the earth"

(*Enter* Mrs. Malaprop, *listening*)

Mrs. Malaprop.   I am impatient to know how the little hussy deports herself.   (*Aside*)

Absolute.   So   pensive, Lydia!—is   then   your warmth abated?

Mrs. Malaprop.   —Warmth abated!—so!—she has been in a passion, I suppose.   (*Aside*)

Lydia.   No—nor ever can while I have life.

Mrs. Malaprop.   An ill-tempered little devil! She'll be in a passion all her life—will she?   (*Aside*)

Lydia.   Think not the idle threats of my ridiculous aunt can ever have any weight with me.

Mrs. Malaprop.   Very dutiful, upon my word!
(*Aside*)

Lydia.   Let her choice be Captain Absolute, but Beverley is mine.

Mrs. Malaprop.   I am astonished at her assurance! —to his face—this is to his face.   (*Aside*)

Absolute.   Thus then let me enforce my suit.

(*Kneeling*)

Mrs. Malaprop.   (*Aside*) Ay, poor young man!— down on his knees entreating for pity!—I can contain no longer.—(*Coming forward*) Why, thou vixen!—I have overheard you.

Absolute.   Oh, confound her vigilance!   (*Aside*)

Mrs. Malaprop.   Captain Absolute, I know not how to apologize for her shocking rudeness.

Absolute.   (*Aside*) So all's safe, I find.—(*Aloud*) I have hopes, madam, that time will bring the young lady——

Mrs. Malaprop.   Oh, there's nothing to be hoped for from her! she's as headstrong as an allegory on the banks of Nile.

Lydia.   Nay, madam, what do you charge me with now?

Mrs. Malaprop.   Why, thou unblushing rebel—

didn't you tell this gentleman to his face that you loved another better?—didn't you say you never would be his?

LYDIA. No, madam—I did not.

MRS. MALAPROP. Good heavens! what assurance! —Lydia, Lydia, you ought to know that lying don't become a young woman!—Didn't you boast that Beverley, that stroller Beverley, possessed your heart? —Tell me that, I say.

LYDIA. 'Tis true, ma'am, and none but Beverley——

MRS. MALAPROP. Hold!—hold, Assurance!—you shall not be so rude.

ABSOLUTE. Nay, pray, Mrs. Malaprop, don't stop the young lady's speech: she's very welcome to talk thus—it does not hurt me in the least, I assure you.

MRS. MALAPROP. You are *too* good, captain—*too* amiably patient—but come with me, miss.—Let us see you again soon, captain—remember what we have fixed.

ABSOLUTE. I shall, ma'am.

MRS. MALAPROP. Come, take a graceful leave of the gentleman.

LYDIA. May every blessing wait on my Beverley, my loved Bev——

MRS. MALAPROP. Hussy! I'll choke the word in your throat!—come along—come along.

(*Exeunt severally;* CAPTAIN ABSOLUTE *kissing his hand to* LYDIA—MRS. MALAPROP *stopping her from speaking*)

SCENE IV: ACRES' *Lodgings*

(ACRES, *as just dressed, and* DAVID)

ACRES. Indeed, David—do you think I become it so?

DAVID. You are quite another creature, believe me, master, by the mass! an' we've any luck we shall see the Devon monkeyrony[1] in all the print-shops in Bath!

ACRES.   Dress does make a difference, David.

DAVID.   'Tis all in all, I think.—Difference! why, an'
you were to go now to Clod Hall, I am certain the old
lady wouldn't know you: Master Butler wouldn't believe his own eyes, and Mrs. Pickle would cry, "Lard
presarve me!" our dairy-maid would come giggling to
the door, and I warrant Dolly Tester, your honour's
favourite, would blush like my waistcoat.—Oons! I'll
hold a gallon, there an't a dog in the house but would
bark, and I question whether Phyllis[2] would wag a
hair of her tail!

ACRES.   Ay, David, there's nothing like polishing.

DAVID.   So I says of your honour's boots, but the
boy never heeds me!

ACRES.   But, David, has Mr. De-la-grace been here?
I must rub up my balancing, and chasing, and boring.[3]

DAVID.   I'll call again, sir.

ACRES.   Do—and see if there are any letters for me
at the post office.

DAVID.   I will.—By the mass, I can't help looking at
your head!—if I hadn't been by at the cooking, I wish
I may die if I should have known the dish again myself.   (*Exit*)

ACRES.   (*Comes forward practising a dancing-step*)
Sink, slide—coupee.—Confound the first inventors of
cotillons![4] say I—they are as bad as algebra to us
country gentlemen.—I can walk a minuet easy enough
when I am forced!—and I have been accounted a good
stick in a country-dance.—Odds jigs and tabors! I
never valued your cross-over to couple—figure in—
right and left—and I'd foot it with e'er a captain in the
county!—but these outlandish heathen allemandes[5]

---

[1] **monkeyrony** macaroni, dandy   [2] **Phyllis** Acres' favorite hunt-
ing hound   [3] **balancing . . . boring** dancing steps   [4] **cotillons**
a dance of French origin   [5] **allemandes** a dance of German
origin

and cotillons are quite beyond me!—I shall never prosper at 'em, that's sure—mine are true-born English legs—they don't understand their curst French lingo! —their *pas*[6] this, and *pas* that, and *pas* t'other!—damn me!—my feet don't like to be called paws! no, 'tis certain I have most Anti-gallican toes!

(*Enter* SERVANT)

SERVANT. Here is Sir Lucius O'Trigger to wait on you, sir.

ACRES. Show him in. (*Exit* SERVANT)

(*Enter* SIR LUCIUS O'TRIGGER)

SIR LUCIUS. Mr. Acres, I am delighted to embrace you.

ACRES. My dear Sir Lucius, I kiss your hands.

SIR LUCIUS. Pray, my friend, what has brought you so suddenly to Bath?

ACRES. Faith! I have followed Cupid's Jack-a-lantern, and find myself in a quagmire at last.—In short, I have been very ill-used, Sir Lucius.—I don't choose to mention names, but look on me as on a very ill-used gentleman.

SIR LUCIUS. Pray what is the case?—I ask no names.

ACRES. Mark me, Sir Lucius, I fall as deep as need be in love with a young lady—her friends take my part —I follow her to Bath—send word of my arrival; and receive answer, that the lady is to be otherwise disposed of.—This, Sir Lucius, I call being ill-used.

SIR LUCIUS. Very ill, upon my conscience.—Pray, can you divine the cause of it?

ACRES. Why, there's the matter; she has another lover, one Beverley, who, I am told, is now in Bath.— Odds slanders and lies! he must be at the bottom of it.

pas dance steps (French)

SIR LUCIUS.   A rival in the case, is there?—and you think he has supplanted you unfairly?

ACRES.   Unfairly! to be sure he has. He never could have done it fairly.

SIR LUCIUS.   Then sure you know what is to be done!

ACRES.   Not I, upon my soul!

SIR LUCIUS.   We wear no swords here,[7] but you understand me.

ACRES.   What! fight him?

SIR LUCIUS.   Ay, to be sure: what can I mean else?

ACRES.   But he has given me no provocation.

SIR LUCIUS.   Now, I think he has given you the greatest provocation in the world. Can a man commit a more heinous offence against another man than to fall in love with the same woman? Oh, by my soul! it is the most unpardonable breach of friendship.

ACRES.   Breach of friendship! ay, ay; but I have no acquaintance with this man. I never saw him in my life.

SIR LUCIUS.   That's no argument at all—he has the less right then to take such a liberty.

ACRES.   Gad, that's true—I grow full of anger, Sir Lucius!—I fire apace! Odds hilts and blades! I find a man may have a deal of valour in him, and not know it! But couldn't I contrive to have a little right on my side?

SIR LUCIUS.   What the devil signifies right, when your honour is concerned? Do you think Achilles, or my little Alexander the Great, ever inquired where the right lay? No, by my soul, they drew their broadswords, and left the lazy sons of peace to settle the justice of it.

ACRES.   Your words are a grenadier's march to my heart! I believe courage must be catching! I certainly do feel a kind of valour rising as it were—a kind of

[7] **no swords here** duelling was forbidden in Bath

courage, as I may say.—Odds flints, pans, and triggers! I'll challenge him directly.

SIR LUCIUS. Ah, my little friend, if I had Blunderbuss Hall here, I could show you a range of ancestry, in the old O'Trigger line, that would furnish the New Rooms;[8] every one of whom had killed his man!—For though the mansion-house and dirty acres have slipped through my fingers, I thank heaven our honour and the family-pictures are as fresh as ever.

ACRES. O, Sir Lucius! I have had ancestors too! every man of 'em colonel or captain in the militia!— Odds balls and barrels! say no more—I'm braced for it. The thunder of your words has soured the milk of human kindness in my breast:—Zounds! as the man in the play[9] says, *I could do such deeds!*

SIR LUCIUS. Come, come, there must be no passion at all in the case—these things should always be done civilly.

ACRES. I must be in a passion, Sir Lucius—I must be in a rage.—Dear Sir Lucius, let me be in a rage, if you love me. Come, here's pen and paper.—(*Sits down to write*) I would the ink were red!—Indite, I say, indite!—How shall I begin? Odds bullets and blades! I'll write a good bold hand, however.

SIR LUCIUS. Pray compose yourself.

ACRES. Come—now, shall I begin with an oath? Do, Sir Lucius, let me begin with a damme.

SIR LUCIUS. Pho! pho! do the thing decently, and like a Christian. Begin now—*Sir*——

ACRES. That's too civil by half.

SIR LUCIUS. *To prevent the confusion that might arise*——

ACRES. Well—

SIR LUCIUS. *From our both addressing the same lady*——

[8] **New Rooms** public assembly halls in Bath [9] **play** *King Lear,* loosely quoted

ACRES. Ay, there's the reason—*same lady*—well

SIR LUCIUS. *I shall expect the honour of your company*——

ACRES. Zounds! I'm not asking him to dinner.

SIR LUCIUS. Pray be easy.

ACRES. Well, then, *honour of your company*——

SIR LUCIUS. *To settle our pretensions*——

ACRES. Well.

SIR LUCIUS. Let me see, ay, King's-Mead-Fields[10] will do—*in King's-Mead-Fields*.

ACRES. So, that's done—Well, I'll fold it up presently; my own crest—a hand and dagger shall be the seal.

SIR LUCIUS. You see now this little explanation will put a stop at once to all confusion or misunderstanding that might arise between you.

ACRES. Ay, we fight to prevent any misunderstanding.

SIR LUCIUS. Now, I'll leave you to fix your own time.—Take my advice, and you'll decide it this evening if you can; then let the worst come of it, 'twill be off your mind to-morrow.

ACRES. Very true.

SIR LUCIUS. So I shall see nothing of you, unless it be by letter, till the evening.—I would do myself the honour to carry your message; but, to tell you a secret, I believe I shall have just such another affair on my own hands. There is a gay captain here who put a jest on me lately at the expense of my country, and I only want to fall in with the gentleman to call him out.

ACRES. By my valour, I should like to see you fight first! Odds life! I should like to see you kill him, if it was only to get a little lesson.

SIR LUCIUS. I shall be very proud of instructing you. Well for the present—but remember now, when

[10] **King's-Mead-Fields** outside the town walls, on the Avon River

you meet your antagonist, do every thing in a mild and agreeable manner.—Let your courage be as keen, but at the same time as polished, as your sword.

(Exeunt severally)

Act IV

Scene I: Acres' *Lodgings*

(Acres *and* David)

David. Then, by the mass, sir! I would do no such thing—ne'er a Sir Lucius O'Trigger in the kingdom should make me fight, when I wasn't so minded. Oons! what will the old lady say, when she hears o't?

Acres. Ah! David, if you had heard Sir Lucius!— Odds sparks and flames! he would have roused your valour.

David. Not he, indeed. I hates such bloodthirsty cormorants. Look'ee, master, if you wanted a bout at boxing, quarter-staff, or short-staff, I should never be the man to bid you cry off: but for your curst sharps[1] and snaps,[2] I never knew any good come of 'em.

Acres. But my honour, David, my honour! I must be very careful of my honour.

David. Ay, by the mass! and I would be very careful of it; and I think in return my honour couldn't do less than to be very careful of me.

Acres. Odds blades! David, no gentleman will ever risk the loss of his honour!

David. I say then, it would be but civil in honour never to risk the loss of a gentleman.—Look'ee, master,

[1] sharps rapiers [2] snaps pistols

this honour seems to me to be a marvellous false friend: ay, truly, a very courtier-like servant.—Put the case, I was a gentleman (which, thank God, no one can say of me); well—my honour makes me quarrel with another gentleman of my acquaintance.—So— we fight. (Pleasant enough that!) Boh!—I kill him— (the more's my luck!) now, pray who gets the profit of it?—Why, my honour. But put the case that he kills me!—by the mass! I go to the worms, and my honour whips over to my enemy.

ACRES. No, David—in that case—odds crowns and laurels! your honour follows you to the grave.

DAVID. Now, that's just the place where I could make a shift to do without it.

ACRES. Zounds! David, you're a coward!—It doesn't become my valour to listen to you.—What, shall I disgrace my ancestors?—Think of that, David —think what it would be to disgrace my ancestors!

DAVID. Under favour, the· surest way of not dis- gracing them, is to keep as long as you can out of their company. Look'ee now, master, to go to them in such haste—with an ounce of lead in your brains—I should think might as well be let alone. Our ancestors are very good kind of folks; but they are the last people I should choose to have a visiting acquaintance with.

ACRES. But, David, now, you don't think there is such very, very, *very* great danger, hey?—Odds life! people often fight without any mischief done!

DAVID. By the mass, I think 'tis ten to one against you!—Oons! here to meet some lion-hearted fellow, I warrant, with his damned double-barrelled swords, and cut-and-thrust pistols! Lord bless us! it makes me tremble to think o't—Those be such desperate bloody- minded weapons! Well, I never could abide 'em!— from a child I never could fancy 'em!—I suppose there an't so merciless a beast in the world as your loaded pistol!

ACRES. Zounds! I *won't* be afraid!—Odds fire and fury! you shan't make me afraid.—Here is the challenge, and I have sent for my dear friend Jack Absolute to carry it for me.

DAVID. Ay, i' the name of mischief, let him be the messenger.—For my part I wouldn't lend a hand to it for the best horse in your stable. By the mass! it don't look like another letter! It is, as I may say, a designing and malicious-looking letter; and I warrant smells of gun-powder like a soldier's pouch!—Oons! I wouldn't swear it mayn't go off!

ACRES. Out, you poltroon! [3] you han't the valour of a grasshopper.

DAVID. Well, I say no more—'twill be sad news, to be sure, at Clod Hall!—but I ha' done. How Phyllis will howl when she hears of it!—Ah, poor bitch, she little thinks what shooting her master's going after! And I warrant old Crop, who has carried your honour, field and road, these ten years, will curse the hour he was born. (*Whimpering*)

ACRES. It won't do, David—I am determined to fight—so get along, you coward, while I'm in the mind.

(*Enter* SERVANT)

SERVANT. Captain Absolute, sir.

ACRES. Oh! show him up. (*Exit* SERVANT)

DAVID. Well, Heaven send we be all alive this time to-morrow.

ACRES. What's that?—Don't provoke me, David!

DAVID. Good-bye, master. (*Whimpering*)

ACRES. Get along, you cowardly, dastardly, croaking raven! (*Exit* DAVID)

(*Enter* CAPTAIN ABSOLUTE)

ABSOLUTE. What's the matter, Bob?

ACRES. A vile, sheep-hearted blockhead! If I hadn't the valour of St. George and the dragon to boot——

[3] **poltroon** coward

ABSOLUTE.   But what did you want with me, Bob?

ACRES.   Oh!—There——

(Gives him the challenge)

ABSOLUTE.   *(Aside)   To   Ensign   Beverley.*—So, what's going on now?—*(Aloud)* Well, what's this?

ACRES.   A challenge!

ABSOLUTE.   Indeed! Why, you won't fight him; will you, Bob?

ACRES.   Egad, but I will, Jack. Sir Lucius has wrought me to it. He has left me full of rage—and I'll fight this evening, that so much good passion mayn't be wasted.

ABSOLUTE.   But what have I to do with this?

ACRES.   Why, as I think you know something of this fellow, I want you to find him out for me, and give him this mortal defiance.

ABSOLUTE.   Well, give it to me, and trust me he gets it.

ACRES.   Thank you, my dear friend, my dear Jack; but it is giving you a great deal of trouble.

ABSOLUTE.   Not in the least—I beg you won't mention it.—No trouble in the world, I assure you.

ACRES.   You are very kind.—What it is to have a friend!—You couldn't be my second, could you, Jack?

ABSOLUTE.   Why no, Bob—not in this affair—it would not be quite so proper.

ACRES.   Well, then, I must get my friend Sir Lucius. I shall have your good wishes, however, Jack?

ABSOLUTE.   Whenever he meets you, believe me.

(Enter SERVANT*)*

SERVANT.   Sir Anthony Absolute is below, inquiring for the captain.

ABSOLUTE.   I'll come instantly.—*(Exit* SERVANT*)* Well, my little hero, success attend you.   *(Going)*

ACRES.   Stay—stay, Jack.—If Beverley should ask

you what kind of a man your friend Acres is, do tell him I am a devil of a fellow—will you, Jack?

ABSOLUTE. To be sure I shall. I'll say you are a determined dog—hey, Bob?

ACRES. Ah, do, do—and if that frightens him, egad, perhaps he mayn't come. So tell him I generally kill a man a week; will you, Jack?

ABSOLUTE. I will, I will; I'll say you are called in the country *Fighting Bob.*

ACRES. Right—right—'tis all to prevent mischief; for I don't want to take his life if I clear my honour.

ABSOLUTE. No!—that's very kind of you.

ACRES. Why, you don't wish me to kill him—do you, Jack?

ABSOLUTE. No, upon my soul, I do not. But a devil of a fellow, hey?   (*Going*)

ACRES. True, true—but stay—stay, Jack,—you may add, that you never saw me in such a rage before—a most devouring rage!

ABSOLUTE. I will, I will.

ACRES. Remember, Jack—a determined dog!

ABSOLUTE. Ay ay, *Fighting Bob!*

(*Exeunt severally*)

SCENE II: MRS. MALAPROP's *Lodgings*

(MRS. MALAPROP *and* LYDIA)

MRS. MALAPROP. Why, thou perverse one!—tell me what you can object to him? Isn't he a handsome man? —tell me that. A genteel man? a pretty figure of a man?

LYDIA. (*Aside*) She little thinks whom she is praising!—(*Aloud*) So is Beverley, ma'am.

MRS. MALAPROP. No caparisons, miss, if you please. Caparisons don't become a young woman. No! Captain Absolute is indeed a fine gentleman!

LYDIA.   (*Aside*) Ay, the Captain Absolute you have seen.

MRS. MALAPROP.   Then he's *so* well bred;—*so* full of alacrity, and adulation!—and has *so much* to say for himself:—in such good language, too! His physiognomy so grammatical! Then his presence is so noble! I protest, when I saw him, I thought of what Hamlet says in the play:—

> Hesperian curls—the front of Job himself!—
> An eye, like March, to threaten at command!—
> A station, like Harry Mercury, new—[1]

Something about kissing—on a hill—however, the similitude struck me directly.

LYDIA.   (*Aside*) How enraged she'll be presently, when she discovers her mistake!

(*Enter* SERVANT)

SERVANT.   Sir Anthony and Captain Absolute are below, ma'am.

MRS. MALAPROP.   Show them up here.—(*Exit* SERVANT) Now, Lydia, I insist on your behaving as becomes a young woman. Show your good breeding, at least, though you have forgot your duty.

LYDIA.   Madam, I have told you my resolution!—I shall not only give him no encouragement, but I won't even speak to, or look at him.

> (*Flings herself into a chair, with her face
> from the door*)

(*Enter* SIR ANTHONY ABSOLUTE *and* CAPTAIN ABSOLUTE)

SIR ANTHONY.   Here we are, Mrs. Malaprop; come to mitigate the frowns of unrelenting beauty,—and

[1] "Hesperian . . . new" misquoted from *Hamlet:* "Hyperion's curls; the front of Jove himself; / An eye like Mars, to threaten and command; / A station like the herald Mercury / New lighted on a heaven-kissing hill"

difficulty enough I had to bring this fellow.—I don't know what's the matter; but if I had not held him by force, he'd have given me the slip.

MRS. MALAPROP. You have infinite trouble, Sir Anthony, in the affair. I am ashamed for the cause!— (*Aside to* LYDIA) Lydia, Lydia, rise, I beseech you! —pay your respects!

SIR ANTHONY. I hope, madam, that Miss Languish has reflected on the worth of this gentleman, and the regard due to her aunt's choice, and *my* alliance.— (*Aside to* CAPTAIN ABSOLUTE) Now, Jack, speak to her.

ABSOLUTE. (*Aside*) What the devil shall I do!— (*Aside to* SIR ANTHONY) You see, sir, she won't even look at me whilst you are here. I knew she wouldn't! I told you so. Let me entreat you, sir, to leave us together! (*Seems to expostulate with his father*)

LYDIA. (*Aside*) I wonder I han't heard my aunt exclaim yet! sure she can't have looked at him!—perhaps their regimentals[2] are alike, and she is something blind.

SIR ANTHONY. I say, sir, I won't stir a foot yet!

MRS. MALAPROP. I am sorry to say, Sir Anthony, that my affluence over my niece is very small.—(*Aside to* LYDIA) Turn round, Lydia: I blush for you!

SIR ANTHONY. May I not flatter myself, that Miss Languish will assign what cause of dislike she can have to my son!—(*Aside to* CAPTAIN ABSOLUTE) Why don't you begin, Jack?—Speak, you puppy—speak!

MRS. MALAPROP. It is impossible, Sir Anthony, she can have any. She will not *say* she has.—(*Aside to* LYDIA) Answer, hussy! why don't you answer?

SIR ANTHONY. Then, madam, I trust that a childish and hasty predilection will be no bar to Jack's happiness.—(*Aside to* CAPTAIN ABSOLUTE) Zounds! sirrah! why don't you speak?

[2] **regimentals** uniforms

LYDIA. (*Aside*) I think my lover seems as little inclined to conversation as myself.—How strangely blind my aunt must be!

ABSOLUTE. Hem! hem! madam—hem!—(*Attempts to speak, then returns to* SIR ANTHONY) Faith! sir, I am so confounded!—and—so—so—confused! I told you I should be so, sir—I knew it.—The—the—tremor of my passion entirely takes away my presence of mind.

SIR ANTHONY. But it don't take away your voice, fool, does it?—Go up, and speak to her directly!

(CAPTAIN ABSOLUTE *makes signs to* MRS. MALAPROP *to leave them together*)

MRS. MALAPROP. Sir Anthony, shall we leave them together?—(*Aside to* LYDIA) Ah! you stubborn little vixen!

SIR ANTHONY. Not yet, ma'am, not yet!—(*Aside to* CAPTAIN ABSOLUTE) What the devil are you at? unlock your jaws, sirrah, or—— (CAPTAIN ABSOLUTE *draws near* LYDIA)

ABSOLUTE. (*Aside*) Now Heaven send she may be too sullen to look round!—I must disguise my voice.— (*Speaks in a low, hoarse tone*) Will not Miss Languish lend an ear to the mild accents of true love? Will not——

SIR ANTHONY. What the devil ails the fellow? why don't you speak out?—not stand croaking like a frog in a quinsy![3]

ABSOLUTE. The—the—excess of my awe, and my—my—modesty quite choke me!

SIR ANTHONY. Ah! your modesty again!—I'll tell you what, Jack, if you don't speak out directly, and glibly too, I shall be in such a rage!—Mrs. Malaprop, I wish the lady would favour us with something more than a side-front.[4]

---

[3] in a quinsy with a sore throat   [4] side-front profile

(MRS. MALAPROP *seems to chide* LYDIA)

ABSOLUTE. (*Aside*) So all will out, I see!—(*Goes up to* LYDIA, *speaks softly*) Be not surprised, my Lydia, suppress all surprise at present.

LYDIA. (*Aside*) Heavens! 'tis Beverley's voice! Sure he can't have imposed on Sir Anthony too!—(*Looks round by degrees, then starts up*) Is this possible?—my Beverley!—how can this be?—my Beverley?

ABSOLUTE. (*Aside*) Ah! 'tis all over.

SIR ANTHONY. Beverley!—the devil—Beverley!—What can the girl mean?—this is my son, Jack Absolute.

MRS. MALAPROP. For shame, hussy! for shame! your head runs so on that fellow, that you have him always in your eyes!—beg Captain Absolute's pardon directly.

LYDIA. I see no Captain Absolute, but my loved Beverley!

SIR ANTHONY. Zounds! the girl's mad!—her brain's turned by reading.

MRS. MALAPROP. O' my conscience, I believe so!—What do you mean by Beverley, hussy?—You saw Captain Absolute before to-day; there he is—your husband that shall be.

LYDIA. With all my soul, ma'am—when I refuse my Beverley——

SIR ANTHONY. Oh! she's as mad as Bedlam![5]—or has this fellow been playing us a rogue's trick!—Come here, sirrah, who the devil are you?

ABSOLUTE. Faith, sir, I am not quite clear myself; but I'll endeavour to recollect.

SIR ANTHONY. Are you my son or not?—answer for your mother, you dog, if you won't for me.

MRS. MALAPROP. Ay, sir, who are you? O mercy! I begin to suspect!——

[5] **Bedlam** Bethlehem Hospital, insane asylum

ABSOLUTE. (*Aside*) Ye powers of impudence, befriend me!—(*Aloud*) Sir Anthony, most assuredly I am your wife's son; and that I sincerely believe myself to be yours also, I hope my duty has always shown.—Mrs. Malaprop, I am your most respectful admirer, and shall be proud to add *affectionate nephew*.—I need not tell my Lydia, that she sees her faithful Beverley, who, knowing the singular generosity of her temper, assumed that name and station, which has proved a test of the most disinterested love, which he now hopes to enjoy in a more elevated character.

LYDIA. (*Sullenly*) So!—there will be no elopement after all!

SIR ANTHONY. Upon my soul, Jack, thou art a very impudent fellow! to do you justice, I think I never saw a piece of more consummate assurance!

ABSOLUTE. Oh, you flatter me, sir—you compliment—'tis my modesty, you know, sir—my modesty that has stood in my way.

SIR ANTHONY. Well, I am glad you are not the dull, insensible varlet you pretended to be, however! —I'm glad you have made a fool of your father, you dog—I am. So this was your *penitence*, your *duty* and *obedience!*—I thought it was damned sudden!—You *never heard their names before*, not you!—*what, the Languishes of Worcestershire*, hey?—*if you could please me in the affair it was all you desired!*—Ah! you dissembling villain!—What!—(*Pointing to* LYDIA) *she squints don't she?—a little red-haired girl!*—hey? —Why, you hypocritical young rascal!—I wonder you a'n't ashamed to hold up your head!

ABSOLUTE. 'Tis with difficulty, sir.—I am confused —very much confused, as you must perceive.

MRS. MALAPROP. O Lud! Sir Anthony!—a new light breaks in upon me!—hey!—how! what! captain, did you write the letters then?—What—am I to thank you for the elegant compilation of *an old weather-*

beaten she-dragon—hey?—O mercy!—was it you that reflected on my parts of speech?

ABSOLUTE. Dear sir, my modesty will be overpowered at last, if you don't assist me.—I shall certainly not be able to stand it!

SIR ANTHONY. Come, come, Mrs. Malaprop, we must forget and forgive;—odds life; matters have taken so clever a turn all of a sudden, that I could find in my heart to be so good-humoured! and so gallant! hey! Mrs. Malaprop!

MRS. MALAPROP. Well, Sir Anthony, since you desire it, we will not anticipate the past!—so mind, young people—our retrospection will be all to the future.

SIR ANTHONY. Come, we must leave them together; Mrs. Malaprop, they long to fly into each other's arms, I warrant!—Jack, isn't the cheek as I said, hey?—and the eye, you rogue?—and the lip—hey? Come, Mrs. Malaprop, we'll not disturb their tenderness—theirs is the time of life for happiness! —*Youth's the season made for joy*[6]—(*Sings*)—hey!— Odds life! I'm in such spirits,—I don't know what I couldn't do!—Permit me, ma'am—(*Gives his hand to* MRS. MALAPROP) Tol-de-rol—'gad, I should like a little fooling myself—Tol-de-rol! de-rol.

       (*Exit, singing and handing*[7] MRS. MALAPROP.

          —LYDIA *sits sullenly in her chair*)

ABSOLUTE. (*Aside*) So much thought bodes me no good.—(*Aloud*) So grave, Lydia!

LYDIA. Sir!

ABSOLUTE. (*Aside*) So!—egad! I thought as much! —that damned monosyllable has froze me!—(*Aloud*) What, Lydia, now that we are as happy in our friends' consent, as in our mutual vows——

LYDIA. (*Peevishly*) Friends' consent indeed!

[6] *Youth . . . joy* a popular song from *The Beggar's Opera*
[7] *handing* escorting by the hand

ABSOLUTE.   Come, come, we must lay aside some of our romance—a little wealth and comfort may be endured after all. And for your fortune, the lawyers shall make such settlements as——

LYDIA.   Lawyers! I hate lawyers!

ABSOLUTE.   Nay, then, we will not wait for their lingering forms, but instantly procure the license, and——

LYDIA.   The license!—I hate license!

ABSOLUTE.   Oh, my love! be not so unkind! (*Kneeling*) Thus let me entreat——

LYDIA.   Psha!—what signifies kneeling, when you know I *must* have you?

ABSOLUTE.   (*Rising*) Nay, madam, there shall be no constraint upon your inclinations, I promise you.— If I have lost your heart—I resign the rest—(*Aside*) 'Gad, I must try what a little spirit will do.

LYDIA.   (*Rising*) Then, sir, let me tell you, the interest you had there was acquired by a mean, unmanly imposition, and deserves the punishment of fraud.— What, you have been treating me like a child!— humouring my romance! and laughing, I suppose, at your success!

ABSOLUTE.   You wrong me, Lydia, you wrong me— only hear——

LYDIA.   So, while I fondly imagined we were deceiving my relations, and flattered myself that I should outwit and incense them all—behold my hopes are to be crushed at once, by my aunt's consent and approbation—and I am myself the only dupe at last!—(*Walking about in a heat*) But here, sir, here is the picture —Beverley's picture! (*Taking a miniature from her bosom*) which I have worn, night and day, in spite of threats and entreaties!—There, sir; (*Flings it to him*) and be assured I throw the original from my heart as easily.

ABSOLUTE.   Nay, nay, ma'am, we will not differ as

to that.—Here, (*Taking out a picture*) here is Miss Lydia Languish.—What a difference!—ay, there is the heavenly assenting smile that first gave soul and spirit to my hopes!—those are the lips which sealed a vow, as yet scarce dry in Cupid's calendar! and there the half-resentful blush, that would have checked the ardour of my thanks!—Well, all that's past?—all over indeed!—There, madam—in beauty, that copy is not equal to you, but in my mind its merit over the original, in being still the same, is such—that—I cannot find it my heart to part with it. (*Puts it up again*)

LYDIA. (*Softening*) 'Tis your own doing, sir—I, I, I suppose you are perfectly satisfied.

ABSOLUTE. O, most certainly—sure, now, this is much better than being in love!—ha! ha! ha!—there's some spirit in this!—What signifies breaking some scores of solemn promises:—all that's of no consequence, you know. To be sure people will say that miss don't know her own mind but never mind that! Or, perhaps, they may be ill-natured enough to hint, that the gentleman grew tired of the lady and forsook her —but don't let that fret you.

LYDIA. There is no bearing his insolence.

(*Bursts into tears*)

(*Re-enter* MRS. MALAPROP *and* SIR ANTHONY ABSOLUTE)

MRS. MALAPROP. Come, we must interrupt your billing and cooing awhile.

LYDIA. This is worse than your treachery and deceit, you base ingrate! (*Sobbing*)

SIR ANTHONY. What the devil's the matter now?— Zounds! Mrs. Malaprop, this is the oddest billing and cooing I ever heard!—but what the deuce is the meaning of it?—I'm quite astonished!

ABSOLUTE. Ask the lady, sir.

MRS. MALAPROP. O mercy!—I'm quite analyzed,

for my part!—Why, Lydia, what is the reason of this?

LYDIA.   Ask the gentleman, ma'am.

SIR ANTHONY.   Zounds! I shall be in a frenzy!— Why, Jack, you are not come out to be any one else, are you?

MRS. MALAPROP.   Ay, sir, there's no more trick, is there?—you are not like Cerberus,[8] three gentlemen at once, are you?

ABSOLUTE.   You'll not let me speak—I say the lady can account for this much better than I can.

LYDIA.   Ma'am, you once commanded me never to think of Beverley again—there is the man—I now obey you: for, from this moment, I renounce him forever.   (*Exit*)

MRS. MALAPROP.   O mercy! and miracles! what a turn here is—why, sure, captain, you haven't behaved disrespectfully to my niece?

SIR ANTHONY.   Ha! ha! ha!—ha! ha! ha!—now I see it. Ha! ha! ha!—now I see it—you have been too lively, Jack.

ABSOLUTE.   Nay, sir, upon my word——

SIR ANTHONY.   Come, no lying, Jack—I'm sure 'twas so.

MRS. MALAPROP.   O Lud! Sir Anthony!—O fy, Captain!

ABSOLUTE.   Upon my soul, ma'am——

SIR ANTHONY.   Come, no excuse, Jack; why, your father, you rogue, was so before you!—the blood of the Absolutes was always impatient.—Ha! ha! ha! poor little Lydia! why, you've frightened her, you dog, you have.

ABSOLUTE.   By all that's good, sir——

SIR ANTHONY.   Zounds! say no more, I tell you. Mrs. Malaprop shall make your peace. You must make his peace, Mrs. Malaprop:—you must tell her 'tis Jack's way—tell her 'tis all our ways—it runs in the

[8] **Cerberus** the three-headed watchdog of Hades

blood of our family! Come away, Jack. Ha! ha! ha!—
Mrs. Malaprop—a young villain!   (*Pushes him out*)
MRS. MALAPROP.   O! Sir Anthony!—O fy, Captain.
                                    (*Exeunt severally*)

SCENE III: *The North Parade*

(*Enter* SIR LUCIUS O'TRIGGER)

SIR LUCIUS.   I wonder where this Captain Absolute
hides himself! Upon my conscience! these officers are
always in one's way in love affairs:—I remember I
might have married Lady Dorothy Carmine, if it had
not been for a little rogue of a major, who ran away
with her before she could get a sight of me! And I
wonder too what it is the ladies can see in them to be
so fond of them—unless it be a touch of the old ser-
pent in 'em, that makes the little creatures be caught,
like vipers, with a bit of red cloth. Ha! isn't this the
captain coming?—faith it is!—There is a probability
of succeeding about that fellow, that is mighty provoking! Who the devil is he talking to?   (*Steps aside*)

(*Enter* CAPTAIN ABSOLUTE)

ABSOLUTE.   (*Aside*) To what fine purpose I have
been plotting! a noble reward for all my schemes,
upon my soul!—a little gipsy!—I did not think her
romance could have made her so damned absurd
either. 'Sdeath, I never was in a worse humour in my
life!—I could cut my own throat, or any other person's,
with the greatest pleasure in the world!

SIR LUCIUS.   Oh, faith! I'm in the luck of it. I never
could have found him in a sweeter temper for my purpose—to be sure I'm just come in the nick! Now to
enter into conversation with him, and so quarrel gen-
teelly.—(*Goes up to* CAPTAIN ABSOLUTE) With regard
to that matter, captain, I must beg leave to differ in
opinion with you.

ABSOLUTE. Upon my word, then, you must be a very subtle disputant:—because, sir, I happened just then to be giving no opinion at all.

SIR LUCIUS. That's no reason. For give me leave to tell you, a man may think an untruth as well as speak one.

ABSOLUTE. Very true, sir; but if a man never utters his thoughts, I should think they might stand a chance of escaping controversy.

SIR LUCIUS. Then, sir, you differ in opinion with me, which amounts to the same thing.

ABSOLUTE. Hark'ee, Sir Lucius; if I had not before known you to be a gentleman, upon my soul, I should not have discovered it at this interview: for what you can drive at, unless you mean to quarrel with me, I cannot conceive!

SIR LUCIUS. I humbly thank you, sir, for the quickness of your apprehension.—(*Bowing*) You have named the very thing I would be at.

ABSOLUTE. Very well, sir; I shall certainly not balk your inclinations.—But I should be glad you would please to explain your motives.

SIR LUCIUS. Pray, sir, be easy; the quarrel is a very pretty quarrel as it stands; we should only spoil it by trying to explain it. However, your memory is very short, or you could not have forgot an affront you passed on me within this week. So, no more, but name your time and place.

ABSOLUTE. Well, sir, since you are so bent on it, the sooner the better; let it be this evening—here, by the Spring Gardens. We shall scarcely be interrupted.

SIR LUCIUS. Faith! that same interruption in affairs of this nature shows very great ill-breeding. I don't know what's the reason, but in England if a thing of this kind gets wind, people make such a pother that a gentleman can never fight in peace and quietness. However, if it's the same to you, I should take it as a particular kindness if you'd let us meet in King's-Mead-Fields, as a little business will call me there about six o'clock, and I may despatch both matters at once.

ABSOLUTE. 'Tis the same to me exactly. A little after six, then, we will discuss this matter more seriously.

SIR LUCIUS. If you please, sir; there will be very pretty small-sword light, though it won't do for a long shot. So that matter's settled, and my mind's at ease!

(*Exit*)

(*Enter* FAULKLAND)

ABSOLUTE. Well met! I was going to look for you. O Faulkland! all the demons of spite and disappointment have conspired against me! I'm so vex'd that if I had not the prospect of a resource in being knocked o' the head by-and-by, I should scarce have spirits to tell you the cause.

FAULKLAND. What can you mean?—Has Lydia changed her mind?—I should have thought her duty and inclination would now have pointed to the same object.

ABSOLUTE. Ay, just as the eyes do of a person who squints: when her love-eye was fixed on me, t'other, her eye of duty, was finely obliqued: but when duty bid her point that the same way, off t'other turned on a swivel, and secured its retreat with a frown!

FAULKLAND. But what's the resource you——

ABSOLUTE. Oh, to wind up the whole, a good-natured Irishman here has—(*Mimicking* SIR LUCIUS) begged leave to have the pleasure of cutting my throat; and I mean to indulge him—that's all.

FAULKLAND. Prithee, be serious!

ABSOLUTE. 'Tis fact, upon my soul! Sir Lucius O'Trigger—you know him by sight—for some affront, which I am sure I never intended, has obliged me to meet him this evening at six o'clock: 'tis on that account I wished to see you; you must go with me.

FAULKLAND.   Nay, there must be some mistake, sure. Sir Lucius shall explain himself, and I dare say matters may be accommodated. But this evening did you say? I wish it had been any other time.

ABSOLUTE.   Why? there will be light enough: there will (as Sir Lucius says) be very pretty small-sword light, though it will not do for a long shot. Confound his long shots.

FAULKLAND.   But I am myself a good deal ruffled by a difference I have had with Julia. My vile tormenting temper has made me treat her so cruelly that I shall not be myself till we are reconciled.

ABSOLUTE.   By heavens! Faulkland, you don't deserve her!

(Enter SERVANT, *gives* FAULKLAND *a letter, and exit)*

FAULKLAND.   Oh, Jack! this is from Julia. I dread to open it! I fear it may be to take a last leave!—perhaps to bid me return her letters, and restore——Oh, how I suffer for my folly!

ABSOLUTE.   Here, let me see.—*(Takes the letter and opens it)* Ay, a final sentence, indeed!—'tis all over with you, faith!

FAULKLAND.   Nay, Jack, don't keep me in suspense!

ABSOLUTE.   Hear then—*(Reads) As I am convinced that my dear Faulkland's own reflections have already upbraided him for his last unkindness to me, I will not add a word on the subject. I wish to speak with you as soon as possible. Yours ever and truly,* JULIA. There's stubbornness and resentment for you!—*(Gives him the letter)* Why, man, you don't seem one whit happier at this!

FAULKLAND.   O yes, I am; but—but—

ABSOLUTE.   Confound your buts! you never hear

anything that would make another man bless himself, but you immediately damn it with a but!

FAULKLAND. Now, Jack, as you are my friend, own honestly—don't you think there is something forward, something indelicate, in this haste to forgive? Women should never sue for reconciliation: that should always come from us. They should retain their coldness till wooed to kindness; and their pardon, like their love, should "not unsought be won."

ABSOLUTE. I have not patience to listen to you! thou'rt incorrigible! so say no more on the subject. I must go to settle a few matters. Let me see you before six, remember, at my lodgings. A poor industrious devil like me, who have toiled, and drudged, and plotted to gain my ends, and am at last disappointed by other people's folly, may in pity be allowed to swear and grumble a little; but a captious sceptic in love, a slave to fretfulness and whim, who has no difficulties but of his own creating, is a subject more fit for ridicule than compassion!   (*Exit*)

FAULKLAND. I feel his reproaches; yet I would not change this too exquisite nicety for the gross content with which he tramples on the thorns of love! His engaging me in this duel has started an idea in my head, which I will instantly pursue. I'll use it as the touch-stone of Julia's sincerity and disinterestedness. If her love proves pure and sterling ore, my name will rest on it with honour; and once I've stamped it there, I lay aside my doubts for ever! But if the dross of selfishness, the alloy of pride, predominate, 'twill be best to leave her as a toy for some less cautious fool to sigh for!   (*Exit*)

Act V

✤

SCENE I: JULIA's *Dressing-Room*

(JULIA *discovered alone*)

JULIA. How this message has alarmed me! what dreadful accident can he mean? why such charge to be alone?—O Faulkland!—how many unhappy moments—how many tears have you cost me.

(*Enter* FAULKLAND [*muffled up in a travelling coat*])

JULIA. What means this?—why this caution, Faulkland?

FAULKLAND. Alas! Julia, I am come to take a long farewell.

JULIA. Heavens! what do you mean?

FAULKLAND. You see before you a wretch whose life is forfeited. Nay, start not!—the infirmity of my temper has drawn all this misery on me. I left you fretful and passionate—an untoward accident drew me into a quarrel—the event is, that I must fly this kingdom instantly. O Julia, had I been so fortunate as to have called you mine entirely, before this mischance had fallen on me, I should not so deeply dread my banishment!

JULIA. My soul is opprest with sorrow at the nature of your misfortune: had these adverse circumstances arisen from a less fatal cause I should have felt strong comfort in the thought that I could now chase from your bosom every doubt of the warm sincerity of my love. My heart has long known no other guardian—I now entrust my person to your honour—we will fly together. When safe from pursuit, my father's will may

be fulfilled—and I receive a legal claim to be the partner of your sorrows and tenderest comforter. Then on
the bosom of your wedded Julia, you may lull your
keen regret to slumbering, while virtuous love, with a
cherub's hand, shall smoothe the brow of upbraiding
thought, and pluck the thorn from compunction.

FAULKLAND. O Julia! I am bankrupt in gratitude!
but the time is so pressing, it calls on you for so hasty a
resolution.—Would you not wish some hours to weigh
the advantages you forego, and what little compensa-
tion poor Faulkland can make you beside his solitary
love?

JULIA. I ask not a moment. No, Faulkland, I have
loved you for yourself: and if I now, more than ever,
prize the solemn engagement which so long has
pledged us to each other, it is because it leaves no
room for hard aspersions on my fame, and puts the
seal of duty to an act of love. But let us not linger.
Perhaps this delay——

FAULKLAND. 'Twill be better I should not venture
out again till dark. Yet am I grieved to think what
numberless distresses will press heavy on your gentle
disposition!

JULIA. Perhaps your fortune may be forfeited by
this unhappy act.—I know not whether 'tis so; but sure
that alone can never make us unhappy. The little I
have will be sufficient to support us; and exile never
should be splendid.

FAULKLAND. Ay, but in such an abject state of life,
my wounded pride perhaps may increase the natural
fretfulness of my temper, till I become a rude, morose
companion, beyond your patience to endure. Perhaps
the recollection of a deed my conscience cannot justify
may haunt me in such gloomy and unsocial fits, that I
shall hate the tenderness that would relieve me, break
from your arms, and quarrel with your fondness!

JULIA. If your thoughts should assume so unhappy

a bent, you will the more want some mild and affectionate spirit to watch over and console you! one who by bearing your infirmities with gentleness and resignation, may teach you so to bear the evils of your fortune.

FAULKLAND. Julia, I have proved you to the quick! and with this useless device I throw away all my doubts. How shall I plead to be forgiven this last unworthy effect of my restless, unsatisfied disposition?

JULIA. Has no such disaster happened as you related?

FAULKLAND. I am ashamed to own that it was pretended; yet in pity, Julia, do not kill me with resenting a fault which never can be repeated: but sealing, this once, my pardon, let me to-morrow, in the face of Heaven, receive my future guide and monitress, and expiate my past folly by years of tender adoration.

JULIA. Hold, Faulkland!—that you are free from a crime, which I before feared to name, Heaven knows how sincerely I rejoice! These are tears of thankfulness for that! But that your cruel doubts should have urged you to an imposition that has wrung my heart, gives me now a pang more keen than I can express.

FAULKLAND. By Heavens! Julia——

JULIA. Yet hear me,—My father loved you, Faulkland! and you preserved the life that tender parent gave me; in his presence I pledged my hand—joyfully pledged it—where before I had given my heart. When, soon after, I lost that parent, it seemed to me that Providence had, in Faulkland, shown me whither to transfer without a pause, my grateful duty, as well as my affection; hence I have been content to bear from you what pride and delicacy would have forbid me from another. I will not upbraid you, by repeating how you have trifled with my sincerity——

FAULKLAND. I confess it all! yet hear——

JULIA. After such a year of trial, I might have flat-

tered myself that I should not have been insulted with
a new probation of my sincerity, as cruel as unnecessary! I now see it is not in your nature to be content
or confident in love. With this conviction—I never will
be yours. While I had hopes that my persevering attention and unreproaching kindness might in time
reform your temper, I should have been happy to have
gained a dearer influence over you; but I will not furnish you with a licensed power to keep alive an incorrigible fault, at the expense of one who never would
contend with you.

FAULKLAND. Nay, but, Julia, by my soul and honour, if after this——

JULIA. But one word more.—As my faith has once
been given to you, I never will barter it with another.
—I shall pray for your happiness with the truest sincerity; and the dearest blessing I can ask of Heaven to
send you will be to charm you from that unhappy temper which alone has prevented the performance of our
solemn engagement. All I request of you is, that you
will yourself reflect upon this infirmity, and when you
number up the many true delights it has deprived
you of, let it not be your least regret, that it lost
you the love of one who would have followed you in
beggary through the world!   (*Exit*)

FAULKLAND. She's gone—forever!—There was an
awful resolution in her manner, that riveted me to
my place.—O fool!—dolt!—barbarian! Cursed as I
am, with more imperfections than my fellow-wretches,
kind Fortune sent a heaven-gifted cherub to my aid,
and, like a ruffian, I have driven her from my side!—
I must now haste to my appointment. Well, my mind
is tuned for such a scene. I shall wish only to become
a principal in it, and reverse the tale my cursed folly
put me upon forging here.—O Love!—tormentor!—
fiend!—whose influence, like the moon's, acting on
men of dull souls, makes idiots of them, but meeting

subtler spirits, betrays their course, and urges sensibility to madness! *(Exit)*

(Enter LYDIA *and* MAID*)*

MAID. My mistress, ma'am, I know, was here just now—perhaps she is only in the next room. *(Exit)*

LYDIA. Heigh-ho! Though he has used me so, this fellow runs strangely in my head. I believe one lecture from my grave cousin will make me recall him. *(Enter* JULIA*)* O Julia, I have come to you with such an appetite for consolation.—Lud! child, what's the matter with you? You have been crying!—I'll be hanged if that Faulkland has not been tormenting you.

JULIA. You mistake the cause of my uneasiness!—Something has flurried me a little. Nothing that you can guess at.—*(Aside)* I would not accuse Faulkland to a sister!

LYDIA. Ah! whatever vexations you may have, I can assure you mine surpass them. You know who Beverley proves to be?

JULIA. I will now own to you, Lydia, that Mr. Faulkland had before informed me of the whole affair. Had young Absolute been the person you took him for, I should not have accepted your confidence on the subject without serious endeavour to counteract your caprice.

LYDIA. So, then, I see I have been deceived by every one! But I don't care—I'll never have him.

JULIA. Nay, Lydia——

LYDIA. Why, is it not provoking? when I thought we were coming to the prettiest distress imaginable, to find myself made a mere Smithfield bargain[1] of at last! There had I projected one of the most sentimental elopements!—so becoming a disguise!—so amiable a ladder of ropes!—Conscious moon—four horses—

[1] **Smithfield bargain** i.e., married for my money

Scotch parson[2]—with such surprise to Mrs. Malaprop —and such paragraphs in the newspapers!—Oh, I shall die with disappointment!

JULIA. I don't wonder at it!

LYDIA. Now—sad reverse!—what have I to expect, but, after a deal of flimsy preparation, with a bishop's license, and my aunt's blessing, to go simpering up to the altar; or perhaps be cried three times in a country church, and have an unmannerly fat clerk ask the consent of every butcher in the parish to join John Absolute and Lydia Languish, *spinster!* Oh that I should live to hear myself called spinster!

JULIA. Melancholy, indeed!

LYDIA. How mortifying, to remember the dear delicious shifts I used to be put to, to gain half a minute's conversation with this fellow! How often have I stole forth, in the coldest night in January, and found him in the garden, stuck like a dripping statue! There would he kneel to me in the snow, and sneeze and cough so pathetically! he shivering with cold and I with apprehension! and while the freezing blast numbed our joints, how warmly would he press me to pity his flame, and glow with mutual ardour!—Ah, Julia, that was something like being in love.

JULIA. If I were in spirits, Lydia, I should chide you only by laughing heartily at you; but it suits more the situation of my mind, at present, earnestly to entreat you not to let a man who loves you with sincerity suffer that unhappiness from your caprice, which I know too well caprice can inflict.

LYDIA. O Lud! what has brought my aunt here?

(*Enter* MRS. MALAPROP, FAG, *and* DAVID)

[2] Scotch parson eloping couples traditionally fled to Scotland where the liberal marriage laws required no "bishop's licence" and no delay for "crying the banns," public announcements of the forthcoming marriage during a series of church services

MRS. MALAPROP. So! so! here's fine work!—here's fine suicide, parricide, and simulation, going on in the fields! and Sir Anthony not to be found to prevent the antistrophe!

JULIA. For Heaven's sake, madam, what's the meaning of this?

MRS. MALAPROP. That gentleman can tell you— 'twas he enveloped the affair to me.

LYDIA. (*To* FAG) Do, sir, will you inform us?

FAG. Ma'am, I should hold myself very deficient in every requisite that forms the man of breeding, if I delayed a moment to give all the information in my power to a lady so deeply interested in the affair as you are.

LYDIA. But quick! quick, sir!

FAG. True, ma'am, as you say, one should be quick in divulging matters of this nature; for should we be tedious, perhaps while we are flourishing on the subject, two or three lives may be lost!

LYDIA. O patience!—do, ma'am, for Heaven's sake! tell us what is the matter?

MRS. MALAPROP. Why, murder's the matter! slaughter's the matter! killing's the matter!—but he can tell you the perpendiculars.

LYDIA. Then, prithee, sir, be brief.

FAG. Why, then, ma'am, as to murder—I cannot take upon me to say—and as to slaughter, or manslaughter, that will be as the jury finds it.

LYDIA. But who, sir—who are engaged in this?

FAG. Faith, ma'am, one is a young gentleman whom I should be very sorry anything was to happen to—a very pretty behaved gentleman! We have lived much together, and always on terms—

LYDIA. But who is this? who? who? who?

FAG. My master, ma'am—my master—I speak of my master.

LYDIA. Heavens! What, Captain Absolute!

MRS. MALAPROP. Oh, to be sure, you are frightened now!

JULIA. But who are with him, sir?

FAG. As the rest, ma'am, this gentleman can inform you better than I.

JULIA. (*To* DAVID) Do speak, friend.

DAVID. Look'ee, my lady—by the mass! there's mischief going on. Folks don't use to meet for amusement with firearms, firelocks,[3] fire-engines, fire-screens, fire-office,[4] and the devil knows what other crackers beside!—This, my lady, I say, has an angry savour.

JULIA. But who is there beside Captain Absolute, friend?

DAVID. My poor master—under favour for mentioning him first. You know me, my lady—I am David —and my master of course is, or was, Squire Acres. Then comes Squire Faulkland.

JULIA. Do, ma'am, let us instantly endeavour to prevent mischief.

MRS. MALAPROP. O fy! it would be very inelegant in us:—we should only participate things.

DAVID. Ah! do, Mrs. Aunt, save a few lives—they are desperately given, believe me.—Above all, there is that bloodthirsty Philistine, Sir Lucius O'Trigger.

MRS. MALAPROP. Sir Lucius O'Trigger? O mercy! have they drawn poor little dear Sir Lucius into the scrape? Why how you stand, girl! you have no more feeling than one of the Derbyshire putrefactions![5]

LYDIA. What are we to do, madam?

MRS. MALAPROP. Why, fly with the utmost felicity, to be sure, to prevent mischief!—Here, friend, you can show us the place?

FAG. If you please, ma'am, I will conduct you.— David, do you look for Sir Anthony. (*Exit* DAVID)

---

[3] **fire-locks** flintlock muskets [4] **fire-office** insurance company
[5] **Derbyshire putrefactions** i.e., objects removed from the petrifying wells of Matlock in Derbyshire

MRS. MALAPROP. Come, girls! this gentleman will exhort us.—Come, sir, you're our envoy—lead the way, and we'll precede.

FAG. Not a step before the ladies for the world!

MRS. MALAPROP. You're sure you know the spot?

FAG. I think I can find it, ma'am; and one good thing is, we shall hear the report of the pistols as we draw near, so we can't well miss them; never fear, ma'am, never fear.   (*Exeunt, he talking*)

SCENE II: *The South Parade*

(*Enter* CAPTAIN ABSOLUTE, *putting his sword under his great-coat*)

ABSOLUTE. A sword seen in the streets of Bath would raise as great an alarm as a mad dog.—How provoking this is in Faulkland!—never punctual! I shall be obliged to go without him at last.—Oh, the devil! here's Sir Anthony! how shall I escape him?

(*Muffles up his face, and makes a circle to go off*)

(*Enter* SIR ANTHONY ABSOLUTE)

SIR ANTHONY. How one may be deceived at a little distance! Only that I see he don't know me, I could have sworn that was Jack!—Hey! Gad's life! it is.— Why, Jack, what are you afraid of? hey—sure I'm right. Why, Jack, Jack Absolute!   (*Goes up to him*)

ABSOLUTE. Really, sir, you have the advantage of me:—I don't remember ever to have had the honour— my name is Saunderson, at your service.

SIR ANTHONY. Sir, I beg your pardon—I took you —hey?—why, zounds! it is—Stay—(*Looks up to his face*) So, so—your humble servant, Mr. Saunderson! Why, you scoundrel, what tricks are you after now?

ABSOLUTE. Oh, a joke, sir, a joke! I came here on purpose to look for you, sir.

SIR ANTHONY. You did! well, I am glad you were so

lucky:—but what are you muffled up so for?—what's this for?—hey?

ABSOLUTE. 'Tis cool, sir, isn't it?—rather chilly somehow:—but I shall be late—I have a particular engagement.

SIR ANTHONY. Stay!—Why, I thought you were looking for me?—Pray, Jack, where is't you are going?

ABSOLUTE. Going, sir?

SIR ANTHONY. Ay, where are you going?

ABSOLUTE. Where am I going?

SIR ANTHONY. You unmannerly puppy!

ABSOLUTE. I was going, sir, to—to—to—to Lydia —sir, to Lydia—to make matters up if I could; and I was looking for you, sir, to—to—

SIR ANTHONY. To go with you, I suppose.—Well, come along.

ABSOLUTE. Oh! zounds! no, sir, not for the world!— I wished to meet with you, sir,—to—to—to—You find it cool, I'm sure, sir—you'd better not stay out.

SIR ANTHONY. Cool!—not at all.—Well, Jack— and what will you say to Lydia?

ABSOLUTE. Oh, sir, beg her pardon, humour her— promise and vow: but I detain you, sir—consider the cold air on your gout.

SIR ANTHONY. Oh, not at all!—not at all! I'm in no hurry.—Ah! Jack, you youngsters, when once you are wounded here (*Putting his hand to* CAPTAIN ABSO- LUTE's *breast*) Hey! what the deuce have you got here?

ABSOLUTE. Nothing, sir—nothing.

SIR ANTHONY. What's this?—here's something damned hard.

ABSOLUTE. Oh, trinkets, sir! trinkets!—a bauble for Lydia.

SIR ANTHONY. Nay, let me see your taste.—(*Pulls his coat open; the sword falls*) Trinkets! a bauble for Lydia!—Zounds! sirrah, you are not going to cut her throat, are you?

ABSOLUTE. Ha! ha! ha!—I thought it would divert you, sir, though I didn't mean to tell you till afterwards.

SIR ANTHONY. You didn't?—Yes, this is a very diverting trinket, truly!

ABSOLUTE. Sir, I'll explain to you.—You know, sir, Lydia is romantic, devilish romantic, and very absurd of course: now, sir, I intend, if she refuses to forgive me, to unsheath this sword, and swear—I'll fall upon its point, and expire at her feet!

SIR ANTHONY. Fall upon a fiddlestick's end!—why, I suppose it is the very thing that would please her.— Get along, you fool!

ABSOLUTE. Well, sir, you shall hear of my success— you shall hear.—*O Lydia!—forgive me, or this pointed steel*—says I.

SIR ANTHONY. *O, booby! stab away and welcome* —says she.—Get along! and damn your trinkets!

(*Exit* CAPTAIN ABSOLUTE)

(*Enter* DAVID, *running*)

DAVID. Stop him! stop him! Murder! Thief! Fire!— Stop fire! Stop fire!—O Sir Anthony—call! call! bid'm stop! Murder! Fire!

SIR ANTHONY. Fire! Murder!—Where?

DAVID. Oons! he's out of sight! and I'm out of breath for my part! O Sir Anthony, why didn't you stop him? why didn't you stop him?

SIR ANTHONY. Zounds! the fellow's mad!—Stop whom? stop Jack?

DAVID. Ay, the captain, sir!—there's murder and slaughter——

SIR ANTHONY. Murder!

DAVID. Ay, please you, Sir Anthony, there's all kinds of murder, all sorts of slaughter to be seen in the fields: there's fighting going on, sir—bloody sword-and-gun fighting!

Sir Anthony. Who are going to fight, dunce?

David. Everybody that I know of, Sir Anthony:— everybody is going to fight, my poor master, Sir Lucius O'Trigger, your son, the captain——

Sir Anthony. Oh, the dog! I see his tricks.—Do you know the place?

David. King's-Mead-Fields.

Sir Anthony. You know the way?

David. Not an inch; but I'll call the mayor—aldermen—constables—churchwardens—and beadles—we can't be too many to part them.

Sir Anthony. Come along—give me your shoulder! we'll get assistance as we go—the lying villain!— Well, I shall be in such a frenzy!—So this was the history of his trinkets! I'll bauble him!   (*Exeunt*)

Scene III: *King's-Mead-Fields*

(*Enter* Sir Lucius O'Trigger *and* Acres, *with pistols*)

Acres. By my valour! then, Sir Lucius, forty yards is a good distance. Odds levels and aims!—I say it is a good distance.

Sir Lucius. Is it for muskets or small field-pieces? Upon my conscience, Mr. Acres, you must leave those things to me.—Stay now—I'll show you.—(*Measures paces along the stage*) There now, that is a very pretty distance—a pretty gentleman's distance.

Acres. Zounds! we might as well fight in a sentrybox! I tell you, Sir Lucius, the farther he is off, the cooler I shall take my aim.

Sir Lucius. Faith! then I suppose you would aim at him best of all if he was out of sight!

Acres. No, Sir Lucius; but I should think forty or eight and thirty yards——

Sir Lucius. Pho! pho! nonsense! three or four feet between the mouths of your pistols is as good as a mile.

ACRES. Odds bullets, no!—by my valour! there is no merit in killing him so near; do, my dear Sir Lucius, let me bring him down at a long shot—a long shot, Sir Lucius, if you love me.

SIR LUCIUS. Well, the gentleman's friend and I must settle that.—But tell me now, Mr. Acres, in case of an accident, is there any little will or commission I could execute for you?

ACRES. I am much obliged to you, Sir Lucius, but I don't understand——

SIR LUCIUS. Why, you may think there's no being shot at without a little risk—and if an unlucky bullet should carry a quietus[1] with it—I say it will be no time then to be bothering you about family matters.

ACRES. A quietus!

SIR LUCIUS. For instance, now—if that should be the case—would you choose to be pickled and sent home?—or would it be the same to you to lie here in the Abbey? I'm told there is very snug lying in the Abbey.

ACRES. Pickled!—Snug lying in the Abbey!—Odds tremors! Sir Lucius, don't talk so!

SIR LUCIUS. I suppose, Mr. Acres, you never were engaged in an affair of this kind before?

ACRES. No, Sir Lucius, never before.

SIR LUCIUS. Ah! that's a pity!—there's nothing like being used to a thing. Pray now, how would you receive the gentleman's shot?

ACRES. Odds files!—I've practised that—there, Sir Lucius—there. (Puts himself in an attitude) A side-front, hey? Odd! I'll make myself small enough? I'll stand edgeways.

SIR LUCIUS. Now—you're quite out—for if you stand so when I take my aim—— (Levelling at him)

ACRES. Zounds! Sir Lucius—are you sure it is not cocked?

[1] quietus discharge, or release (from life)

SIR LUCIUS. Never fear.

ACRES. But—but—you don't know—it may go off of its own head!

SIR LUCIUS. Pho! be easy.—Well, now if I hit you in the body, my bullet has a double chance—for if it misses a vital part of your right side, 'twill be very hard if it don't succeed on the left!

ACRES. A vital part.

SIR LUCIUS. But, there—fix yourself so—(*Placing him*)—let him see the broad-side of your full front—there—now a ball or two may pass clean through your body, and never do any harm at all.

ACRES. Clean through me!—a ball or two clean through me!

SIR LUCIUS. Ay—may they—and it is much the genteelest attitude into the bargain.

ACRES. Look'ee! Sir Lucius—I'd just as lieve be shot in an awkward posture as a genteel one; so, by my valour! I will stand edgeways.

SIR LUCIUS. (*Looking at his watch*) Sure they don't mean to disappoint us—Hah!—no, faith—I think I see them coming.

ACRES. Hey!—what!—coming!——

SIR LUCIUS. Ay.—Who are those yonder getting over the stile?

ACRES. There are two of them indeed!—well—let them come—hey, Sir Lucius!—we—we—we—we—won't run.

SIR LUCIUS. Run!

ACRES. No—I say—we *won't* run, by my valour!

SIR LUCIUS. What the devil's the matter with you?

ACRES. Nothing—nothing—my dear friend—my dear Sir Lucius—but I—I—I don't feel quite so bold, somehow, as I did.

SIR LUCIUS. O fy!—consider your honour.

ACRES. Ay—true—my honour. Do, Sir Lucius,

edge in a word or two every now and then about my honour.

SIR LUCIUS. (*Looking*) Well, here they're coming.

ACRES. Sir Lucius—if I wa'n't with you, I should almost think I was afraid.—If my valour should leave me! Valour will come and go.

SIR LUCIUS. Then pray keep it fast, while you have it.

ACRES. Sir Lucius—I doubt it is going—yes—my valour is certainly going!—it is sneaking off!—I feel it oozing out as it were at the palms of my hands!

SIR LUCIUS. Your honour—your honour.—Here they are.

ACRES. O mercy!—now—that I was safe at Clod Hall! or could be shot before I was aware!

(*Enter* FAULKLAND *and* CAPTAIN ABSOLUTE)

SIR LUCIUS. Gentleman, your most obedient.— Hah!—what, Captain Absolute!—So, I suppose, sir, you are come here, just like myself—to do a kind office, first for your friend—then to proceed to business on your own account.

ACRES. What, Jack!—my dear Jack!—my dear friend!

ABSOLUTE. Hark'ee, Bob, Beverley's at hand.

SIR LUCIUS. Well, Mr. Acres—I don't blame your saluting the gentleman civilly.—(*To* FAULKLAND) So, Mr. Beverley, if you'll choose your weapons, the captain and I will measure the ground.

FAULKLAND. My weapons, sir!

ACRES. Odds life! Sir Lucius, I'm not going to fight Mr. Faulkland; these are my particular friends.

SIR LUCIUS. What, sir, did you not come here to fight Mr. Acres?

FAULKLAND. Not I, upon my word, sir.

SIR LUCIUS. Well, now, that's mighty provoking! But I hope, Mr. Faulkland, as there are three of us come on purpose for the game, you won't be so cantankerous as to spoil the party by sitting out.

ABSOLUTE. O pray, Faulkland, fight to oblige Sir Lucius.

FAULKLAND. Nay, if Mr. Acres is so bent on the matter——

ACRES. No, no, Mr. Faulkland;—I'll bear my disappointment like a Christian.—Look'ee, Sir Lucius, there's no occasion at all for me to fight; and if it is the same to you, I'd as lieve let it alone.

SIR LUCIUS. Observe me, Mr. Acres—I must not be trifled with. You have certainly challenged somebody —and you came here to fight him. Now, if that gentleman is willing to represent him—I can't see, for my soul, why it isn't just the same thing.

ACRES. Why no—Sir Lucius—I tell you, 'tis one Beverley I've challenged—a fellow, you see, that dare not show his face!—if he were here, I'd make him give up his pretensions directly!

ABSOLUTE. Hold, Bob—let me set you right—there is no such man as Beverley in the case.—The person who assumed that name is before you; and as his pretensions are the same in both characters, he is ready to support them in whatever way you please.

SIR LUCIUS. —Well, this is lucky.—Now you have an opportunity—

ACRES. What, quarrel with my dear friend, Jack Absolute?—not if he were fifty Beverleys! Zounds! Sir Lucius, you would not have me so unnatural.

SIR LUCIUS. Upon my conscience, Mr. Acres, your valour has oozed away with a vengeance!

ACRES. Not in the least! Odds backs and abettors! I'll be your second with all my heart—and if you should get a quietus, you may command me entirely. I'll get you snug lying in the Abbey here; or pickle you, and send you over to Blunderbuss Hall, or anything of the kind, with the greatest pleasure.

Sir Lucius.   Pho! pho! you are little better than a coward.

Acres.   Mind, gentlemen, he calls me a coward; coward was the word, by my valour!

Sir Lucius.   Well, sir?

Acres.   Look'ee, Sir Lucius, 'tisn't that I mind the word coward—coward may be said in joke.—But if you had called me a poltroon, odds daggers and balls——

Sir Lucius.   Well, sir?

Acres.   I should have thought you a very ill-bred man.

Sir Lucius.   Pho! you are beneath my notice.

Absolute.   Nay, Sir Lucius, you can't have a better second than my friend Acres.—He is a most determined dog—called in the country, Fighting Bob.—He generally kills a man a week—don't you, Bob?

Acres.   Ay—at home!

Sir Lucius.   Well, then, captain, 'tis we must begin —so come out, my little counsellor—(*Draws his sword*)—and ask the gentleman, whether he will resign the lady, without forcing you to proceed against him?

Absolute.   Come on then, sir—(*Draws*); since you won't let it be an amicable suit, here's my reply.

(*Enter* Sir Anthony Absolute, David, Mrs. Malaprop, Lydia, *and* Julia)

David.   Knock 'em all down, sweet Sir Anthony; knock down my master in particular; and bind his hands over to their good behaviour!

Sir Anthony.   Put up, Jack, put up, or I shall be in a frenzy—how came you in a duel, sir?

Absolute.   Faith, sir, that gentleman can tell you better than I; 'twas he called on me, and you know, sir, I serve His Majesty.

Sir Anthony.   Here's a pretty fellow; I catch him

going to cut a man's throat, and he tells me he serves His Majesty!—Zounds! sirrah, then how durst you draw the King's sword against one of his subjects?

ABSOLUTE. Sir! I tell you, that gentleman called me out, without explaining his reasons.

SIR ANTHONY. Gad! sir, how came you to call my son out, without explaining your reasons?

SIR LUCIUS. Your son, sir, insulted me in a manner which my honour could not brook.

SIR ANTHONY. Zounds! Jack, how durst you insult the gentleman in a manner which his honour could not brook?

MRS. MALAPROP. Come, come, let's have no honour before ladies—Captain Absolute, come here—How could you intimidate us so?—Here's Lydia has been terrified to death for you.

ABSOLUTE. For fear I should be killed, or escape, ma'am?

MRS. MALAPROP. Nay, no delusions to the past— Lydia is convinced; speak, child.

SIR LUCIUS. With your leave, ma'am, I must put in a word, here: I believe I could interpret the young lady's silence. Now mark——

LYDIA. What is it you mean, sir?

SIR LUCIUS. Come, come, Delia, we must be serious now—this is no time for trifling.

LYDIA. 'Tis true, sir; and your reproof bids me offer this gentleman my hand, and solicit the return of his affections.

ABSOLUTE. O! my little angel, say you so?—Sir Lucius, I perceive there must be some mistake here, with regard to the affront which you affirm I have given you. I can only say that it could not have been intentional. And as you must be convinced that I should not fear to support a real injury, you shall now see that I am not ashamed to atone for an inadvertency —I ask your pardon.—But for this lady, while honoured with her approbation, I will support my claim against any man whatever.

SIR ANTHONY. Well said, Jack, and I'll stand by you, my boy.

ACRES. Mind, I give up all my claim—I make no pretensions to anything in the world; and if I can't get a wife without fighting for her, by my valour! I'll live a bachelor.

SIR LUCIUS. Captain, give me your hand: an affront handsomely acknowledged becomes an obligation; and as for the lady, if she chooses to deny her own hand-writing, here——   (*Takes out letters*)

MRS. MALAPROP. O, he will dissolve my mystery! —Sir Lucius, perhaps there's some mistake—perhaps I can illuminate——

SIR LUCIUS. Pray, old gentlewoman, don't interfere where you have no business.—Miss Languish, are you my Delia or not?

LYDIA. Indeed, Sir Lucius, I am not.

          (*Walks aside with* CAPTAIN ABSOLUTE)

MRS. MALAPROP. Sir Lucius O'Trigger—ungrateful as you are—I own the soft impeachment—pardon my blushes, I am Delia.

SIR LUCIUS. You Delia—pho! pho! be easy.

MRS. MALAPROP. Why, thou barbarous vandyke— those letters are mine.—When you are more sensible of my benignity—perhaps I may be brought to en-courage your addresses.

SIR LUCIUS. Mrs. Malaprop, I am extremely sensi-ble of your condescension; and whether you or Lucy have put this trick on me, I am equally beholden to you.—And, to show you I am not ungrateful, Captain Absolute, since you have taken that lady from me, I'll give you my Delia into the bargain.

ABSOLUTE. I am much obliged to you, Sir Lucius; but here's my friend, Fighting Bob, unprovided for.

SIR LUCIUS. Hah! little Valour—here, will you make your fortune?

ACRES. Odds wrinkles! No.—But give me your hand, Sir Lucius, forget and forgive; but if ever I give you a chance of pickling me again, say Bob Acres is a dunce, that's all.

SIR ANTHONY. Come, Mrs. Malaprop, don't be cast down—you are in your bloom yet.

MRS. MALAPROP. O Sir Anthony—men are all barbarians. (*All retire but* JULIA *and* FAULKLAND)

JULIA. (*Aside*) He seems dejected and unhappy—not sullen; there was some foundation, however, for the tale he told me—O woman! how true should be your judgment, when your resolution is so weak!

FAULKLAND. Julia!—how can I sue for what I so little deserve? I dare not presume—yet Hope is the child of Penitence.

JULIA. Oh! Faulkland, you have not been more faulty in your unkind treatment of me than I am now in wanting inclination to resent it. As my heart honestly bids me place my weakness to the account of love, I should be ungenerous not to admit the same plea for yours.

FAULKLAND. Now I shall be blest indeed.

SIR ANTHONY. (*Coming forward*) What's going on here?—So you have been quarrelling too, I warrant? Come, Julia, I never interfered before; but let me have a hand in the matter at last.—All the faults I have ever seen in my friend Faulkland seemed to proceed from what he calls the delicacy and warmth of his affection for you.—There, marry him directly, Julia; you'll find he'll mend surprisingly!

(*The rest come forward*)

SIR LUCIUS. Come, now I hope there is no dissatisfied person, but what is content; for as I have been disappointed myself, it will be very hard if I have not the satisfaction of seeing other people succeed better.

ACRES. You are right, Sir Lucius.—So, Jack, I wish you joy.—Mr. Faulkland the same.—Ladies,—come now, to show you I'm neither vexed nor angry, odds tabors and pipes! I'll order the fiddles in half an hour to the New Rooms—and I insist on your all meeting me there.

SIR ANTHONY. 'Gad! sir, I like your spirit; and at night we single lads will drink a health to the young couples, and a husband to Mrs. Malaprop.

FAULKLAND. Our partners are stolen from us, Jack —I hope to be congratulated by each other—*yours* for having checked in time the errors of an ill-directed imagination, which might have betrayed an innocent heart; and *mine,* for having, by her gentleness and candour, reformed the unhappy temper of one, who by it made wretched whom he loved most, and tortured the heart he ought to have adored.

ABSOLUTE. Well, Jack, we have both tasted the bitters, as well as the sweets of love; with this difference only, that you always prepared the bitter cup for yourself, while I——

LYDIA. Was always obliged to me for it, hey! Mr. Modesty?——But come, no more of that—our happiness is now as unalloyed as general.

JULIA. Then let us study to preserve it so: and while Hope pictures to us a flattering scene of future bliss, let us deny its pencil those colours which are too bright to be lasting.—When hearts deserving happiness would unite their fortunes, Virtue would crown them with an unfading garland of modest hurtless flowers; but ill-judging Passion will force the gaudier rose into the wreath, whose thorn offends them when its leaves are dropped!   (*Exeunt omnes*)

EPILOGUE

SPOKEN BY MRS. BULKLEY

LADIES, for you—I heard our poet say—
He'd try to coax some moral from his play:
"One moral's plain," cried I, "without more fuss;
Man's social happiness all rests on us:
Through all the drama—whether damn'd or not—
Love gilds the scene, and women guide the plot.
From every rank obedience is our due—
D'ye doubt?—The world's great stage shall prove it
    true."

The cit,[1] well skill'd to shun domestic strife,
Will sup abroad; but first he'll ask his wife:
John Trot, his friend, for once will do the same,
But then—he'll just step home to tell his dame.

The surly squire at noon resolves to rule,
And half the day—Zounds! madam is a fool!
Convinced at night, the vanquished victor says,
Ah, Kate! you women have such coaxing ways.

The jolly toper chides each tardy blade,
Till reeling Bacchus calls on Love for aid:
Then with each toast he sees fair bumpers swim,
And kisses Chloe on the sparkling brim!

Nay, I have heard that statesmen—great and wise—
Will sometimes counsel with a lady's eyes!
The servile suitors watch her various face,
She smiles preferment, or she frowns disgrace,
Curtsies a pension here—there nods a place.

Nor with less awe, in scenes of humbler life,
Is view'd the mistress, or is heard the wife.
The poorest peasant of the poorest soil,

[1] cit city-dweller

The child of poverty, and heir to toil,
Early from radiant Love's impartial light
Steals one small spark to cheer this world of night:
Dear spark! that oft through winter's chilling woes
Is all the warmth his little cottage knows!

The wandering tar, who not for years has press'd
The widow'd partner of his day of rest,
On the cold deck, far from her arms removed,
Still hums the ditty which his Susan loved;
And while around the cadence rude is blown,
The boatswain whistles in a softer tone.

The soldier, fairly proud of wounds and toil,
Pants for the triumph of his Nancy's smile!
But ere the battle should he list her cries,
The lover trembles—and the hero dies!
That heart, by war and honour steel'd to fear,
Droops on a sigh, and sickens at a tear!

But ye more cautious, ye nice-judging few,
Who give to beauty only beauty's due,
Though friends to love—ye view with deep regret
Our conquests marr'd, our triumphs incomplete,
Till polish'd wit more lasting charms disclose,
And judgment fix the darts which beauty throws!
In female breasts did sense and merit rule,
The lover's mind would ask no other school;
Shamed into sense, the scholars of our eyes,
Our beaux from gallantry would soon be wise;
Would gladly light, their homage to improve,
The lamp of knowledge at the torch of love!

BIBLIOGRAPHY

LIFE

Moore, Thomas, *Memoirs of the Life of Richard Brinsley Sheridan* (London, 1825).

Rhodes, R. C., *Harlequin Sheridan* (London, 1933).

TEXTS

Rhodes, R. C., *The Plays and Poems of Richard Brinsley Sheridan* (3 vols., Oxford, 1928).

Purdy, R. L., ed., *The Rivals* (Oxford, 1935). Prints parallel texts of two versions of the play: (1) The Larpent Manuscript, preserving the text as performed on the first night, and (2) the first published edition, the text as successfully revised after its initial failure.

CRITICISM

Bernbaum, Ernest, *The Drama of Sensibility* (Boston, 1915).

Krutch, Joseph Wood, *Comedy and Conscience after the Restoration* (New York, 1949).

Nettleton, G. F., *English Drama of the Restoration and Eighteenth Century* (New York, 1914).

Nicol, Allardyce, *A History of Late Eighteenth Century Drama* (Cambridge, Eng., 1927).

BACKGROUND

Barbeau, Alfred, *Life and Letters at Bath in the Eighteenth Century* (New York, 1904).

LeFanu, William, ed., *Betsy Sheridan's Journal. Letters from Sheridan's Sister, 1784–1786 and 1786–1790* (New Brunswick, N.J., 1960).

Price, Cecil, ed., *Letters* (3 vols., Oxford, 1966).